H. D. M. (Henry Donald Maurice) Spence-Jones

**Cloister life in the days of Cœur de Lion**

H. D. M. (Henry Donald Maurice) Spence-Jones

**Cloister life in the days of Cœur de Lion**

ISBN/EAN: 9783741139185

Manufactured in Europe, USA, Canada, Australia, Japa

Cover: Foto ©Thomas Meinert / pixelio.de

Manufactured and distributed by brebook publishing software
(www.brebook.com)

H. D. M. (Henry Donald Maurice) Spence-Jones

**Cloister life in the days of Cœur de Lion**

# CLOISTER LIFE IN THE DAYS OF CŒUR DE LION.

Lincoln Cathedral
&
Exchequer Gate.

# CLOISTER LIFE in the days of Cœur de Lion

BY

*Reginald Maurice*

## THE VERY REV. H. D. M. SPENCE D.D.

DEAN OF GLOUCESTER

AUTHOR OF "DREAMLAND IN HISTORY," ETC.

*WITH ILLUSTRATIONS BY HERBERT RAILTON AND A. QUINTON*

LONDON

ISBISTER & COMPANY LIMITED

PHILADELPHIA: J. B. LIPPINCOTT COMPANY

1892

# CONTENTS.

## LINCOLN.

## BURY ST. EDMUNDS.

## TEWKESBURY.

*b*

## EVESHAM.

## OSRIC, KING OF NORTHUMBRIA.

## LA GRANDE CHARTREUSE.

# LIST OF ILLUSTRATIONS.

### By HERBERT RAILTON and A. QUINTON.

[*Erratum*—Cut on page 9, for "Angel Choir" read "Choir."]

# Cloister Life in the days of Cœur de Lion.

B

# Lincoln

## CHAPTER I.

### An Ideal Monk.

It was in the days of Cœur de Lion and his great father, the Angevin Henry II., and his predecessor King Stephen, that the monastic orders did their noblest work among us. It was a rough and cruel age, an age of great crimes and of great repentances.

Never, perhaps, has a more crushing disaster overtaken a whole people than when the Norman Conquest overwhelmed the great and wealthy Anglo-Saxon race—when the entire island, its fertile lands, its towns, its treasure, its people, rich and poor, became the spoil of the conquerors. A few hundred Normans became suddenly rich and powerful; many thousand Saxons were plunged into poverty, misery, servitude.

Long years passed before peace and prosperity were restored to hapless, conquered England. It is true that, after several generations, conquerors and conquered were mingled together and produced a nation the like of which the world had never seen before—a nation which gradually

grew in strength and power, in ability and endurance, grew
into the mighty English race of to-day.   But the early years
of the making of this great
people were, indeed, years of
cruel trial and awful suffering.

The reigns of Stephen,
Henry II., Cœur de Lion, and
John, were years of untold
misery for thousands.

The great repentance on
the part of some of the conquerors helped materially to
produce that wonderful array
of homes of peace—monas-
teries, nunneries, stately abbeys, wonderful cathedrals—
a mighty array of homes, many
gone, some picturesque ruins,
not a few with us still, devoted
to the service of God and the
help of the suffering and the
down-trodden — an array of
stately buildings and sacred
societies such as the world had
never seen before and will
probably never see again.*
Men, many of them noble by
birth, rich and powerful, overwhelmed by the sight of the
great misery around them, devoted themselves and their
lives to relieving, as best they could, the misery of their

*Statue of
King Stephen*

*From the West
front of Wells
Cathedral.*

* In Stephen's reign of nineteen years 115 monasteries were built, and 113
were added to these during the reign of Henry II., making a total of 228 monasteries built in these two reigns.

neighbours, to lifting this burden of the unspeakable woe
they had brought on the land they had conquered. The
monastic orders in these reigns attained, perhaps, their
loftiest ideal, and did right noble work in their generation.
They were not faultless by any means, but many of the
monks well deserved the title of Saint.

I will try and reproduce some scenes from the life of one
of these true great ones, which may be taken as a fair specimen of the views and aspirations of not a few among the vast
army of devoted " religious " who lived in these times—
the days of the birth-throes of our English people.

Far away from England, among the mountains of Savoy
—in that country now so well known among the seekers after
a lost health, in the neighbourhood of pleasant, sunny Aix-
les-Bains—about the middle of the twelfth century, lived a boy
of a noble race, who from early days had been brought up
by men who dwelt in monasteries. A chance visit to the
monastery of the Grande Chartreuse, in company with the
prior of the house in which he was living, determined the
young Hugh of Avalon's future career. The weird beauty
of the situation of the lonely house of St. Bruno and his
companions, the towering rocks which overhung the group of
cells, the far-reaching sombre pine-forests with their melancholy and ceaseless music, which surrounded the little valley
of prayer, the remoteness from all human habitations, the
stern grave life lived by the solitaries devoted to God,
inspired the young seeker after righteousness and truth with
a passionate longing to share in what he felt was a beautiful
life. After a lengthened novitiate the young noble took the
final vows of a Carthusian monk, and in the course of a long
and stormy career this early love never grew cold, never
faded.

The rule of St. Bruno was ascetic even to painful severity ;
meat was forbidden, and only the plainest and coarsest food

sanctioned; each brother of the order lived alone, never meeting his companions save in the chapel or on rare occasions. His bed-furniture was a rough blanket, a pillow, and a skin; his dress a horsehair shirt covered *outside* with linen worn night and day, with the white cloak of the order—in early times a sheepskin. This life of solitary meditation and prayer might go on for the professed brother for years. It might cease at any moment, as he was bound by vows of obedience never to be questioned. At the bidding of his " general " he was liable to be sent on the most distant and perilous mission, for these men owned neither country nor race; all men were their brethren.

As we have said, the eleventh and twelfth centuries were especially an age of cruelty and misrule, of greedy conquerors and hapless conquered—an age in which helpless, defenceless multitudes lived under the rule of merciless masters, generally indifferent to suffering, when law was the feeblest and most untrustworthy stay of right.* In this stern, pitiless age, the monasteries—very numerous in England—and their inhabitants were the only power that could be relied on to exercise any real check upon these cruel and oppressive forces. By the mouth of the monk, in this age of violence and conquest, spoke the voice of the helpless, defenceless people, and their voice, thus uttered, compelled a hearing. It was with these " homes of prayer " that a man who in good earnest meant to serve God and to help his down-trodden neighbour associated himself, or, in other words, " any high effort in those days to be thorough and religious took the shape of monastic discipline and rule."

A peculiar but an effective training for a great mind with a noble ideal was the life of such a monastery as the

---

* Compare Dean Church, "Anselm," chap. ii.—viii., &c.

Grande Chartreuse in the twelfth century.* "The governing thought was that the life there was a warfare, and the monastery was a camp or barrack; there was continued drill and exercise, fixed times, appointed tasks, hard fare, stern punishment; watchfulness was to be incessant, obedience prompt and absolute, no man was to have a will of his own, no man was to murmur."

In such a life as this the young Savoyard noble spent twenty happy years—years so happy that in after time, when he had become one of the earth's great ones, when he had a palace for his home instead of a naked cell, and wore rich clothing in place of the rough haircloth and sheep's-wool cloak, he would come back to a solitary English "Chartreuse" as to a retreat of perfect enjoyment.

"When the cares of the great world fell heavily upon the great monk-statesman, Hugh would often come to his little Carthusian cell† for rest of mind and body, and on coming there would pitch away his grand dress and jump into his sheepskin as we moderns put on our shooting-jackets."

For twenty years Brother Hugh, the Carthusian, was a monk of the great house built in the solitudes of the Savoy Alps. Far and wide his name was whispered abroad as the most gifted monk of the famous order. His life had proved for him the most admirable discipline. The unswerving obedience had taught him how best to rule and influence others; the rigid discipline, the hard fare, the stern gray life had taught him to set its true value upon luxury and magnificence; very poor and tawdry seemed to him the prizes of the world which men spend their existence in striving after. His keen and powerful intellect grew with

---

* Church's "Anselm," chap. iii.

† Froude's "A Bishop of the Twelfth Century" ("Short Studies on Great Subjects").

years as he performed his solitary duties at the Chartreuse, varied with the public tasks allotted him by his superiors.

The traditionary cell of Brother Hugh is still shown at the Grande Chartreuse; it is marked with the letter **F** in the ancient Gothic cloister, and bears the motto—

"𝔅eati qui esuriunt et sitiunt justitiam quoniam ipsi saturabuntur."

The learned Carthusian who describes the cell remarks that the original monastery was built of wood, and was destroyed by fire, but that scarcely any change or modification has taken place in the arrangement and details of the holy house and its cells since Hugh's time.

It is virtually the same quaint little dwelling, provided with the same rough and scanty furniture, containing, too, the same divisions, and situated in the same position in the cloister. The view from the narrow cell garden, still called his, is the picture, literally unchanged, which represented Hugh's world during his many years of monk-life at the Grande Chartreuse. The solitary who occupies "Hugh's cell" still looks out on the gloomy mountain, clothed with tier upon tier of pines, whose dark plumy foliage changes but little in colour with the varying seasons.

Above the mighty pine forest, the huge, gray rock-wall of the Grand Som, rising up abruptly three thousand feet, leaves only a narrow strip of blue sky above to light up the sombre melancholy of the Carthusian landscape. This grave and lonely prospect ever before the monk's eyes was part of a stern and special education, but it was a training which has done its work in the world's story, and it resulted in a life which it is wiser simply to record, and perhaps to wonder at with an ungrudging admiration, than to criticise.

Hugh was almost in middle life when a wonderful and unexpected opening for a new, strange service presented itself to him—a new service which brought him into close contact

Lincoln Cathedral.

The Angel Choir.

with two of the most famous kings in our many-coloured English story.

The dealings of Hugh the Carthusian monk with Henry II. the great Plantagenet king, with Richard the Lionhearted, and later with John Lackland, tell us something of the strong influence for good exercised over these mighty, irresponsible mediæval monarchs by a loving and sympathising Christian monk, whose education had taught him never to be afraid of the mightiest, whose training in a great and solemn monastery had made him "capable of the highest things, content—as living before Him with whom there is neither high nor low—to minister to the humblest." *

And the story of these dealings of the monk Hugh in the latter half of his noble life with these kings possesses another and a very different charm; it lifts up for a moment the veil which hangs over these memorable royal lives—the veil of years, the veil of many traditions of glory as of shame—and we are brought absolutely face to face for a brief moment with Henry Plantagenet,† the greatest and most powerful monarch of the age; face to face with Richard the Lion-hearted, the bravest champion in Christendom, the hero of our boyish memories; face to face with John Lackland, the perjured, the murderer, the abhorred and detested John, who sleeps, however, as he prayed to sleep, in holy company in the gorgeous shrine at Worcester.

---

\* Church, "Anselm," chap. xiv.

† "Seven centuries off, thou wilt see *King Henry II.* visibly there, in all his glory, in some high presence-chamber, a vivid, noble-looking man, with grizzled beard, in glittering uncertain costume, with earls round him, and bishops and dignitaries, in the like." . . . "*Cœur de Lion*, not a theatrical popinjay, with greaves and steel cap on, but a man living upon victuals. Thou brave Richard! . . . he loved a man, and knew one when he saw him!" . . . "*John Lackland*, a blustering, dissipated, human figure, with a kind of blackguard quality air, in cramoisy velvet, with much plumage and fringing amid numerous other human figures of the like, riding abroad with hawks, talking noisy nonsense; . . . a shabby Lackland as he was!"—*Carlyle*, "Past and Present: *The Ancient Monk*," chap. i.

This brilliant chapter in the monk's story came about as follows. It was about the year of our Lord 1174 that Henry II., after the strange scenes of submission he had gone through in the matter of the murder of Thomas à Becket, determined to introduce the Carthusian order into England. It was noble on the part of the great Angevin king to desire to strengthen a mighty institution like that of the monastic orders, with whom he had waged a life-and-death contest and had been signally worsted. But the Plantagenet recognised the almost limitless influence of these orders, and, like a true patriot statesman, desired to invigorate and make more perfect a power which might so materially aid the future progress of the people he loved so well.

The first settlement of the Carthusians at Witham, near Frome, was attended with grave dissensions between the monks and the tenants of the monks' lands. The stranger Carthusians, disheartened with their difficulties, were preparing to return to their native Savoy mountains, when Hugh, whose splendid devotion and great abilities were recognised in the order, was directed to take charge of the new English community as their prior. It was sorely against his will that he left his cell in his beloved Grande Chartreuse ; but with the true monk obedience was the first, the paramount consideration. By the good management of the new prior and the help of the king, who recognised his ability and unbending integrity, the differences were soon arranged, the fame of Witham Priory rapidly grew. It became a favourite place of pilgrimage. The monks were even said to work miracles. The wise prior, however, thought little of these, considering that the only miracle which a monk could really work, and which was worth speaking about, was holiness of life. His biographer, his faithful friend and companion, Brother Adam, subsequently Abbot of Eynsham, relates how at this period of his life he (Adam) observed how the Prior Hugh worked many miracles, but he paid no heed to them, and so he lived for eleven more years a quiet, simple, earnest life, governing his little community, training himself unconsciously for higher and more difficult work.

One day Prior Hugh received a royal command from Eynsham, near royal Woodstock, to attend a great council. King Henry II. told him the canons of Lincoln had chosen him, and that he, the king, fully approved the choice, to be bishop of the great see of Remigius ; the late bishop, Walter de Coutances, had been promoted to the archiepiscopal see of Rouen. Very unwillingly and interposing many questions before his acceptance, Hugh the monk became Hugh the bishop. He was then more than fifty years old ; thirty-two or thirty-three years of training in the stern ascetic school of unquestioning obedience and ceaseless work had well fitted him for the great part he was now to play in public life.

Brother Adam, in his account of this part of the historic life of the monk-bishop, tells us comparatively little of the stirring public events which made the period of Hugh's episcopate so memorable. Most of our readers are well acquainted with the charming romance of "Ivanhoe," perhaps the most widely read of the writings of the great Scottish novelist and poet ; the period described in the story of "Ivanhoe" corresponded to that in which Hugh was bishop of Lincoln. The grand crusade, the absence from England of Richard Cœur de Lion, the captivity and return of the Lion-hearted, the plots and treachery of Prince John—of all these stirring events the monk Hugh was a spectator ; nay, more, he was a prominent actor in not a few of them.* Brother Adam tells

* See Froude "A Bishop of the Twelfth Century," drawn from the "Magna Vita S. Hugonis Episcopi Lincolnensis," edited by Rev. J. F. Dimock. Mr. Froude speaks of this biography of "Brother Adam" as containing the most vivid picture which has come down to us of England as it then was, and of the first Plantagenet kings. The "Magna Vita S. Hugonis" was first printed in the

us little of these; church questions, the ecclesiastical disputes in which Hugh took a part, curious details of his beloved master's life, traits of his lovable character—these are the things which Adam delights to tell us of; they are what concerned him, and he thought they would interest his readers—dwellers for the most part in lonely cloisters—much more than recitals of State policy, more than the sorrows and joys, more than the marriages and deaths of kings and princes, more than war, though the war was for the possession of Jerusalem and the Holy Places. I daresay he was right. Men and women do not change much, and Walter Scott is read by thousands, while Hume and even Froude can only count their students by hundreds. So we must be grateful for gossip-loving Adam's memoirs, especially when our biographer takes us in the course of his narrative, as now and again he does, into the august presence of the Plantagenet kings, Henry II., Cœur de Lion, and shifty John.

His hero-master Hugh—I call him advisedly "hero," for a more heroic soul than that of Hugh of Avalon never dwelt in a frail and delicate body—was evidently a trusted friend and counsellor of two at least of these famous monarchs. Not long after the monk's elevation it happened that at Lincoln a rich prebendal stall fell vacant. King Henry II. wanted it for one of his courtiers, and wrote his views on the matter to Bishop Hugh, thinking he had only to express his wish to obtain the stall for his friend. Hugh at once wrote back to the king, "that these stalls were for priests, not for courtiers." The king was very angry, and peremptorily sent for Hugh. Henry II. was then residing at his favourite palace of Woodstock, and the Carthusian bishop was at Dorchester, a place in that day in the far-reaching diocese of distant Lincoln.

seventeenth century; editor, Dom le Vasseur; and again was edited by Dom le Couteulx. For this study of mine, I have also used and quoted from the recently written exhaustive and scholarly "Vie de S. Hugues," par un Religieux de la Grande Chartreuse (Montreuil, 1890).

Hugh was introduced into the presence of Henry as he sat, with his courtiers round him, under a tree. The king before whom the monk-bishop stood, whose power he was quietly defying, was no ordinary man. He was not only one of the wisest, but was perhaps the most powerful prince in Christendom. He was absolute sovereign of England, and across the seas his dominions embraced almost the half of what is now known as France. He was closely connected by marriage and relationship with the emperor and the kings of France and Arragon. He was the head of the house of the Norman kings of Sicily, and was heir of the Christian king of Jerusalem. His glory and power were acknowledged not only throughout the western but also in the eastern world. But Hugh the monk looked on the face of his mighty sovereign, who ever since he had come to England had been his friend, unabashed. It seemed but a trifling favour that the king asked from him, but Hugh felt that to grant it would be an injury to a far greater king than Henry Plantagenet.

"The bishop approached—no one rose or spoke. He saluted the king; there was no answer. Then Hugh drew near; gently pushing aside an earl who was sitting at Henry's side, he took his place. Silence still continued. At last Henry, looking up, called for a needle and thread. He had hurt a finger of his left hand; it was wrapped with a strip of linen, the end was loose, and the king began to sew. The bishop watched him through a few stitches, and then with the utmost composure said to him, 'Quam similis es modo cognatis tuis de Falesiâ.'—'Your Majesty reminds me now of your cousins of Falaise.' Henry at once saw the allusion and, the chronicler tells us, was convulsed with laughter. Then turning to his court, 'Do you see what this facetious visitor means? He is referring to my ancestress, the mother of the Conqueror, Arletta, the Tanner of Falaise's daughter.

Falaise, you know, is famous for its leather work. He says when I was stitching the linen round my finger I was showing my descent.'

"Then turning to the monk-bishop he asked him how he could treat his king with such scant courtesy as to refuse him the small favour in the matter of the stall at Lincoln. 'I know myself,' answered Hugh gravely, 'to be indebted to your Highness for my late promotion, but I considered your Highness's soul would be in danger if I was found wanting in the discharge of my duties, so I resisted an improper attempt on your part to appropriate a stall in my cathedral.'" [*]

Henry was too wise a man not to know the bishop was right. He had had many other experiences too of Hugh, so when the first flush of anger at being crossed in his will had faded away, he recognised what a source of strength to throne and altar was such a fearless, honest man. The king asked no more for the disputed stall.

[*] "Vie de S. Hugues;" also Froude.

# CHAPTER II.

## The Monk and the King.

Hugh's friend, King Henry II., died two years after the scene at Woodstock just related. Cœur de Lion succeeded. The old friendship with the father was continued to the son, whom he probably had often seen and talked with in Henry II.'s lifetime. Our monk-bishop seems to have loved dearly the "Lion-Heart," forgiving and making allowances for the many mistakes and faults of the great crusader, and only seeing his splendid qualities and his generous chivalry.

During the fifteen years of his episcopate, A.D. 1185—1200, we catch sight of our "ideal monk" playing continually the part of a true statesman in the stormy days of King Richard, standing perpetually between the high-handed oppressor and the oppressed; we see him always the same fearless, simple figure, restlessly working for others, as much at home at the court of the warrior king of England, surrounded by his mailed barons and captains, as in the sad precincts of a leper hospital, or among his rough workmen who were building for him his stately cathedral on the hill of Lincoln, or alone on the marshes with wild birds, over which he acquired a strange influence. It would almost seem as though, like King Solomon in the Arabian story, he possessed the

D

Cathedral from the
Pottergate

language of birds, and could talk with them and tell them his kind, sweet thoughts.

In most of the ancient as well as in the more modern paintings and sculptures in which St. Hugh is represented, a large white swan is introduced close to the figure of the saint. The story of the friendship of St. Hugh and this wild creature is interesting. Shortly after his acceptance of the see of Lincoln, he saw in a Lincolnshire mere an enormous white swan, which was strangely attracted to this friend of dumb creatures. The wild white swan attached himself to the bishop, and was with difficulty ever after separated from his master. His biographer tells us how the swan constantly watched over Hugh while he slept, and would allow no one to disturb him.

This peculiar power which he exercised over wild birds and animals, it has been noticed, was possessed by other practical, holy men. St. Cuthbert, the favourite saint of the North, whose bones rest in that grand minster which looks down at Durham on the Wear, and St. Guthlac, the holy solitary, whose noble monument we still wonder at when we gaze at the beautiful ruin of Crowland, both possessed this influence over wild birds and untamed creatures.

With the sick and dying he was singularly winning and tender. "Pardon, blessed Jesus," exclaims his chaplain Adam, "pardon the unhappy soul of him who tells the story. When I saw my master (Bishop Hugh) touch those livid faces; when I saw him kiss the sightless eyes, or eyeless sockets, I shuddered with disgust. But Hugh said to me that these afflicted ones were flowers of Paradise, pearls in the coronet of the eternal King waiting for the coming of their Lord who in His own time would change their forlorn bodies into the likeness of His own glory." He would visit these poor scarred lepers, wash their cruel sores with his own hands, kiss them, pray with them, comfort them.

He had a remarkable love too for the last sad rites with which our holy religion lays the dead to rest, often taking out of the hands of his priests and chaplains the solemn beautiful service over the corpse.

On one of these occasions we read how, when he was at Rouen with King Richard, he was summoned to the royal table. "The king," he said in reply to the court messenger, "must not wait for me. He had better dine without me than that I should leave my Master's work undone."

He found time in his busy, happy life to share in the work of church building—a work which in the ages when the Plantagenets ruled attained an excellence never attained before, and perhaps never to be reached again. Hugh found the Norman cathedral of Remigius at Lincoln half in ruins, the result of the earthquake of the year 1185. He busied himself, with the zeal he ever threw into the work which lay before him, to raise money and prepare designs for a noble minster. The choir and eastern transept of the present matchless cathedral were completed in Hugh's lifetime, and a beautiful tradition is still with us which tells how the monk-bishop not only assisted in the planning of the wondrous pile, but now and again worked with his own hands among the masons and carpenters as they fashioned the stones and carved the beams of the great church.

We have already spoken of his love for Cœur de Lion. It was in the year 1197 that a serious rupture took place between the king and the bishop. Richard commanded that a contingent of men-at-arms from the see of Lincoln should be sent to help him in one of his perpetual foreign wars. Hugh resisted, and said the liberties of the see which he had sworn to defend forbade any subsidies of men and money being levied for foreign service. Other bishops yielded the point and provided the subsidies, but Hugh stoutly resisted, defying even the royal threat of confiscation. The impetuous

Chapter House
Lincoln

Richard was deeply incensed. Hugh determined to see him; he left England, and found Cœur de Lion at Roche d'Andeli, hearing mass in the church. The interview between the angry sovereign and the fearless monk was a curious one.

" Richard was sitting in a great chair at the opening into the choir; on either side of him were the bishops of Durham and Ely. Hugh came near and bowed to the sovereign. Richard frowned and turned away. ' Kiss me, my lord king,' said the bishop: the kiss was the usual greeting between the sovereign and the spiritual peer. The king turned away still more pointedly. ' Kiss me, my lord,' said the monk again, grasping Cœur de Lion by the vest, and shaking him. Angrily Richard replied, ' Non meruisti.'— ' Thou hast not deserved it.' ' I have deserved it,' said Hugh, still grasping the royal dress. Had he shown the slightest fear, probably the ' Lion-Heart' would have ordered him into captivity; but who could resist such marvellous audacity? The royal kiss was given. Bishop Hugh passed up to the altar, and became at once absorbed in the service, King Richard curiously watching him. After the mass the two old friends were reconciled, the bishop gaining, strange to say, his point." The king's words were remembered in after days, when he had left for ever the scenes of his glories and troubles : " If all bishops were like my lord of Lincoln, not a prince among us could lift his head against them."[*]

The two friends—seemingly so unlike—never met again in this world. Hugh had returned to England, but soon started again for the Continent to try once more to influence King Richard, who, being in sore need of money, persisted in making unjust demands on England. But before he reached Angers Sir Gilbert de Lacy met him with the sad news of the restless prince's death. He had received a mortal wound from an arrow at the siege of Châlus.

[*] " Vic de S. Hugues," livre ii. ch. vii. Froude.

Hugh arrived at Fontevraud on Palm Sunday, just in time to look on the coffin of his loved " Lion-Heart." *

Monument to Henry II. and Richard I. and their Queens.   Formerly at Fontevraud.
(*By permission of Mr. J. C. Wall.*)

* The body of Richard was laid by the side of his father, Henry II., in the Abbey of Fontevraud.   The "lion-heart" was bequeathed to the Canons of Rouen, who enshrined it in "silver and gold" and placed it in their cathedral. This precious relic was discovered in 1838 (July 31), in a cavity formed in the lateral wall of the choir.   It was enclosed within two leaden boxes, the interior one lined with a very thin plate of silver, on which were engraved :—

✠ HIC ∶ JACET ∶
COR ∶ RICAR
DI ∶ REGIS ∶
ANGLORUM

The story of Adam, the chaplain, takes us next into the presence chamber of John Lackland, now king of England. But we miss the old playful, fearless love which existed between the last two sovereigns, Henry and Richard, and our monk. Hugh knew John too well, and we only now see the stern, grave ascetic. John Lackland, in some points of his character, resembled the French king, Louis XI.; when his dark heart was plotting some selfish crime, a dread of the unseen, a certain fearful foreboding of judgment, would come over him. The evil prince believed and trembled, but still went on quietly arranging for and then committing the deadly sin. When dying he was asked where he wished his body to be laid. The king replied that he committed his body and soul to the care of God and St. Wulfstan, the saint-bishop of Worcester. His wish was carefully complied with, and the splendid tomb of the Plantagenet, though the choir of Worcester has been reconstructed since the interment of King John, is still hard by the resting-place of the saint in whose protection he trusted at the last, and to whose care he committed his body.

One of John's first thoughts after his brother Cœur de Lion's death was to secure the friendship of the monk-bishop Hugh, with whose pure and beautiful character Prince John was well acquainted. The new king sent for Hugh, who at once obeyed the summons. They met at Chinon, and travelled together to Fontevraud. King John would pray with Hugh at the graves of Henry and Richard.

There the fearless Carthusian told John what his life should now be, dwelling on the awful responsibility of a sovereign. The king was deeply moved, and made many fair promises for the future.

The heart was much shrunken, and "had the appearance of a reddish-coloured leaf, dry and bent round at the ends." It was wrapped in a sort of taffety of a greenish colour. It now reposes beneath a stately tomb with an effigy of the king resting on it, on the south side of the choir of Rouen Cathedral.—(" *The Tombs of the Kings of England.*" By J. Charles Wall. 1891.)

E

" See," said the prince, " what I always wear next my heart," showing to the monk-bishop a curious gem set in gold. " This stone was given to one of my royal ancestors, who was told by the donor it would ever protect the Plantagenet who wore it from evil and harm."

" Ah," said Hugh, " you must trust in something more mighty than in a magic stone; there is a living, precious Stone —our dear Lord Jesus; trust in Him."

In the porch of Fontevraud Abbey—where the father and brother against whom John had sinned so deeply were sleeping their last sleep—there was a famous sculptured representation of the Last Judgment, one of those terrible and beautiful realistic designs over which the mediæval artist loved to spend half a lifetime. In one corner of the judgment scene, on the left hand, was depicted a group of sad condemned souls, each wearing a crown and holding a sceptre. " Keep," said the stern Carthusian, " this awful picture, prince, ever before your eyes, remembering what a sad destiny is reserved for the hapless souls of kings who were called in life to rule over others, and yet were unable to rule their own evil passions. In eternity these will become slaves to demons."

" Nay," said John, taking Hugh's hand and leading him across the abbey porch; " see there that group of crowned redeemed ones robed in white on the Judge's right hand; I mean to follow the example of those righteous princes. It is in their blessed company I shall be found on the Judgment Day."

Alas, Hugh's sad estimate of King John was the true one ; and when the wise monitor was removed, as he soon was, from earthly courts and earthly kings the story of John Lackland's life proved the saddest and the most evil which the historian of the kings of England has had to record.

# CHAPTER III.

## The Death of Hugh of Lincoln.

The scene with John at the graves of Fontevraud took place not long before the close of Hugh's busy, noble life. The monk-bishop was prostrated by sudden weakness. He was scarcely an old man, and might well have looked forward still to years of splendid usefulness, but death came quickly.

Hugh had paid, in the year following Richard's death, a last visit to his beloved Grande Chartreuse, and in his old haunts seemingly was as strong as ever, but on his way home his strength failed. Resting at his London house in the old Temple, he felt the end was come. Had not the great churchman, the patriot statesman, the loving monk, left his life's hopes and dreams buried in the royal tomb at Fontevraud? Hugh was willing to live on, it seems, and to work on as long as his Master pleased, but the joy of living was quenched, the sunny hopefulness of existence seems to have been darkened for ever when Richard Cœur de Lion died.

He lay for some time in great suffering quietly fading away. Among his notable visitors was King John, whom he cared little for; the wicked prince ever had a reluctant and lingering attachment to the loyal, devoted friend of his dead father and brother. Hugh knew that for him the end was at hand, and with calm cheerfulness prepared for it. There was little to do. His whole life had been a preparation for the other and grander state of being. Fear of death had no place in his heart. "We should be indeed unhappy," * he was heard to say, "if we were not allowed to die at all." He told his friends the exact spot in his great minster church where he wished to be buried, and so waited quietly for death.

In those long-drawn-out, weary last days in the old Temple, he was several times heard whispering to the divine Master he had loved for so many work-filled years, "My God, the fight has surely lasted long enough. Thy dear will be done, but it will be a great boon to me if Thou wilt put an end to this struggle."

In Archbishop Lanfranc's monastic regulations, which generally represent the rule of the great houses in England and on the Continent in the best days of monk-life, elaborate and minute rules are laid down about the treatment of the dying. When the brother entered into his agony, a haircloth was spread on the floor of the cell, ashes were sprinkled over it, a cross was made on the ashes, and on this the dying brother was laid. "The whole convent was summoned by sharp, repeated blows on a board. All who heard it—unless service in the church was going on—were to gather near and repeat the Penitential Psalms, and so, in the presence of the house, amid the low muttered whispers of prayer and psalm, in sackcloth and ashes, the monk of God died." So, writes Dean Church, died Anselm, and that master-builder, Gundulf of Rochester; so passed away Bruno, the founder of the Carthusian order, and unnumbered other known and unknown saints and holy men, whose names we believe are written in the Book of God.

Hugh well remembered this strange custom, and when very weak—the fever which consumed him ever increasing—

* "Magna Vita," livre v. ch. xix. "Vie de S. Hugues," livre iv. ch. vii.

The Death of St. Bruno, Founder of the Order and Builder of La Grande Chartreuse.
(*From the picture by Lesueur in the Louvre.*)

he felt the great peace at last was near. So the dying bishop said to his chaplain, "Now get ready the holy ashes and spread them in a cross-form on the floor beside my bed, and when you see the end is close, take me up and lay me on them."

The agony grew harder to bear. "God of mercy," he kept murmuring, "give me rest." His faithful chaplain heard him. "The beating of your pulse, my lord," he said, "tells us you will soon be resting and at peace." "Ah," whispered the dying monk-bishop, "blessed are they whom the Last Judgment will bring into changeless peace." "The Day of Judgment," replied his friend, "is now dawning upon you. God will very soon now let you lay aside the weary burden of the flesh." "No," replied the Bishop Hugh— ever the accurate theologian even in that hour of mortal weakness—"no, you are wrong. The day of my death will not be the Day of Judgment, but it will be for me a day of grace and mercy."

On the last afternoon of the noble life the bystanders heard Hugh praying, but for others. One of them asked him to pray God that a true successor might follow him in his work. The hearing of the saint was growing dull. Hence was the request for the bishop's prayer repeated. At last Hugh murmured, "Yes, God grant this," and then he spoke no more audible words. Shortly afterwards he partly turned, and raising his hand he mutely blessed the cross of ashes strewn by his side and seemed to motion his weeping friends to lay him at once on this rough bed. He was obeyed and tenderly placed on the ashes.

It was now night. Some of the clerks of St. Paul's Cathedral, who were present with the dean, began to say the office of Compline, and while they were chanting the "Nunc dimittis" the great soul of Hugh went home.* "One of the most beautiful spirits," writes the most eloquent of our historians, by no means a blind admirer of the mo- nastic system, "that was ever incarnated in human clay."

He was buried, as he desired, in that stately but as yet unfinished minster of his on the hill of Lincoln. Round his grave gathered, indeed, a strange and motley group. The King of England, John Lackland, helped to carry the bier

* "Vie de S. Hugues," livre iv. ch. vii.  "Magna Vita," livre v. ch. xviii.

of the well-loved monk; by his side, helping with the sad burden, was the King of Scotland. Among the mourners were many bishops and abbots, earls and barons; and conspicuous among them was a company of poor Jews, wishing to show their loving homage to one who, in an age conspicuous for its fierce persecution of the chosen race, had ever helped them to bear the sad and grievous burden of their hunted, harassed life.

They laid him as he wished in the dress in which, fourteen years before, he had been consecrated bishop. The vestments had been kept in the sacristy at Lincoln against this day, his birthday into real life. They were all, from the sandals to the mitre, perfectly simple in character. He had chosen them himself, and on the day of his elevation to the great office, when he laid them aside after the imposing ceremony, he told his friends when they were to be put on again.

Some eighty years later (A.D. 1280) the Angel Choir of Lincoln Minster, designed by master hands as a fitting resting-place for the loved Carthusian bishop, was ready for the reception of the splendid shrine which held the body of Hugh. The shrine was of beaten gold and was placed in the stately resting-place in the presence of the greatest of our English kings. Queen Philippa, standing by King Edward I., watched this last solemn act.

For more than two centuries and a half the golden shrine and its sacred contents remained the most precious treasure of the noblest of our English cathedrals. It was ruthlessly swept away in the stress and storm of the year of grace 1549, in an age when men chose to forget the great traditions of the past, and the beautiful story of one of the makers of England.

From that sad day, in the Angel Choir only a black marble slab marks the grave where it was supposed the remains of Hugh were re-interred. The grave was opened

in late days, and Canon Venables, the scholar Precentor of
Lincoln, has told us how, beneath the marble slab, a stone
coffin was found.    Within this *loculus* was another coffin of
lead.    It was opened; no body or skeleton was found, only
a decaying mass of linen and silken vestments.    These were
curiously arranged to simulate the shape of a human body.
Not even a fragment of bone was there, but it was evident
from the stains on the side of the leaden coffin that a corpse
had once reposed in it.    Were not these " vestments " in all
human probability the ones which St. Hugh had so carefully
laid by for his last long sleep ?

Such was the man, nurtured and educated by the
monastic orders of the twelfth century.    It may be said he
was a rare and exceptional example.    It is true that Hugh
of the Chartreuse was an especially gifted man, but the
spirit which lived in the monk of our little study guided and
governed the lives of uncounted men and women in that
fierce age of trial.    Surely the school which could train such
noble servants for their country, their Church, and their
God, can never be lightly spoken of, but must ever hold an
honoured place among the makers of our England.

> " Servants of God ! or sons
> Shall I not call you ? because
> Not as servants ye know
> Your Father's innermost mind,
>         *        *        *
> Yours is the praise, if mankind
> Hath not as yet in its march
> Fainted, and fallen, and died !
>     *        *        *        *
> Then in such hour of need
> Of your fainting dispirited race,
> Ye, like angels, appear
> Radiant with armour divine.
> Beacons of hope, ye appear !
> Languor is not in your heart,
> Weakness is not in your word,
> Weariness not on your brow."

# Bury St Edmunds.

## CHAPTER I.

### EDMUND, KING AND MARTYR.

OUTSIDE the walls of the great monasteries, in the twelfth century, comparatively few could read with ease; there was scarcely any literature:* a few poems, a rare chronicle, the Bible, the Missal, the Breviary and "Hours," made up the bulk of the books of the dark ages; few of the mighty castles of the Norman conquerors, the vast ruins of which we still gaze at and admire, boasted of a library whose scanty shelves held any books besides these works, and even these few were little used save by the monk or chaplain who served the castle and its baron as almoner.

* This by no means exaggerates the general ignorance of the early Middle Ages. For instance, as late as the fourteenth century, Du Guesclin, Constable of France, one of the foremost men of the age, could neither read nor write, and John, King of Bohemia, was equally ignorant; the Emperor Frederick Barbarossa (end of twelfth century) could not read; Philippe le Hardi, King of France, son of St. Louis (thirteenth century), was likewise unable to read. For many centuries it was rare for any layman of whatever rank to know how to sign his name. A few signatures to deeds appear, however, in the fourteenth century. On the scarcity of books at this time (centuries twelve and thirteen) and the enormous price they fetched, see Hallam, "Middle Ages," iii., ix., 1, and Robertson's "Charles V.," introduction, vol. 1, note x.; "Sismondi," tom. 5, &c.

F

Within, however, the home of prayer, things were different; there not a few of the fathers were learned men, many
could read and write and speak fluently several tongues ;
English (Anglo-Saxon), Norman-French, Provençal-French
(the langues d'Oc and d'Oil), and even dialects of these, were
to not a few very familiar; and above all, Latin was to every
monk who dreamed of rising to any post of honour and
dignity in his house a well-known tongue. Greek before the
fifteenth century was little studied ; * Hebrew and Oriental
languages still less. The words and thoughts of the old
Church writers, and of the Roman classic writers, were read
and pondered over by young and old in their long hours of
study or recreation.† But there was no " public " outside
their walls who cared for books—hardly any one in the court
or camp of the Norman and Plantagenet kings, very few
merchants or burghers in London or Winchester or
Gloucester, who were interested in literature of any kind—
scarcely any indeed who could read fluently enough to study
with pleasure.

This want of an outside world who could read and take
an interest in their written thoughts, their poetry, their
theology, their diaries, their stories, no doubt generally acted
as an effectual barrier to original writing on the part of the
monks of the famous religious houses in the days of the
early Plantagenets. There was no demand for their compositions, nothing to spur them on to what we should call
literary exertion. There were numberless scholars, but they
for the most part contented themselves with reading,
pondering over, copying again and again the Scriptures,

---

* I am speaking here, of course, in the main of England, and English and
Norman monasteries.

† Jocelin de Brakelonda, in his little chronicle of domestic incidents, quotes
often Horace and Virgil, Cicero, Seneca, Terence and Lucan, &c., in such a
way as to show us how familiar he was with the thoughts and expressions of
these writers.

their missals and the great masterpieces of a by-gone age, seldom, however, adding fresh thoughts to the old store.

Hence the singular barrenness of all monastic records. There are many of these with us still,* some carefully printed and edited in the scholarly series of the Master of the Rolls, others remaining in our great libraries in manuscript. These give us ample and elaborate information as to the names and functions of the various officers or obedienciaries of the more important monasteries; their cartularies supply us with detailed information as to the lands and farms, their chronicles and histories give a little, but very little, contemporary history; they record a few of the royal and more important visits to the house, they relate much of the disputes of the monks with the bishops of the see and with the royal officials, mentioning year by year the chief changes in the persons of the principal officers of the society, occasionally dwelling on individual delinquencies. They recount with fair accuracy too the progress of building and altering and restoring the church and cloisters, granges, schools, farms, abbot and prior's lodgings, infirmaries, campaniles, refectories, and such like, registering also frequently the more important gifts of sacred vestments and furniture. And all this with apparently studied brevity, with painful dryness; rarely do we find anything of what we should call human interest in these chronicles and cartularies.

The truth was, had these scribe-monks been at the pains to record the impressions of their inner lives, their thoughts, aspirations, longings, fears, desires, imaginings, searchings of heart, no one in those days would have cared to read or hear them. So we find volumes of dry official matters, business-like records, and nothing more; many a detail of

---

* The thirteenth and following centuries were especially prolific in monastic chronicles. These are of inestimable value to all compilers of history. What we have such scant knowledge is of the inner life of the monasteries.

inestimable value to the antiquary and the historian, but, alas! little that would interest the ordinary thoughtful reader.

Owing to this sad dearth of writings which possess any general interest among the monkish compilations of the twelfth, thirteenth, and fourteenth centuries which are preserved among us, we know comparatively little of the real life which was led in these great homes of prayer, where the men were trained who exercised such vast influence over men's souls in those rough, rude times. "Bells tolled to prayers; and men of many humours, various thoughts, chanted vespers and matins, and round the little islet of their life rolled for ever the illimitable ocean, tinting all things with its eternal hues and reflexes, making strange prophetic music! How silent now! all departed; clean gone."* How we long to get glimpses of this deep buried time!

Amid the mass of *reliquiæ* of monastic writings, here and there we come upon a fragment which throws a little light upon the "life;" perhaps none so vivid, so bright, though, as the light thrown by a chronicle written by a monk of St. Edmundsbury who lived in the days of Cœur de Lion, his father Henry II. and his brother John Lackland.

This little chronicle, written in the last quarter of the twelfth century, completely lifts up the veil which hangs over monastic life in the days of Cœur de Lion. Jocelin of Brakelonda, the chronicler, was a learned, simple-hearted monk, who during a long series of years held various responsible offices in the great house of St. Edmundsbury, among others—in his younger days—that of chaplain for some six years to the abbot. It is a kind of private diary, or rather extracts from a private diary, reaching over many years. Probably Jocelin in later years re-copied certain portions or extracts of his original work, selecting what seemed to him

* Carlyle.

the memoranda bearing on the more important incidents which had happened in the house, and in which he had for the most part taken a share. His memoirs tell us of the little intrigues among the monks, of their work, of their thoughts one of another, of their difficulties, of their longing after the higher life, of their faults and mistakes; nothing is concealed. He wrote it all down just as it happened, quite naturally and simply, in his rough, monkish Latin, not, however, without a certain charm of manner.

Some half a century ago Carlyle came across this diary, and our great writer and thinker, struck with the vivid, life-like picture it contained of the rugged monk who is its subject (Abbot Samson), used Jocelin's little story* as a striking evidence in favour of that theory of hero-worship on which he loved to insist. Carlyle was "writing under a sense of the hopelessness of democracy, and the belief that the heroic ruler, gifted with the necessary courage and insight, was the sole hope whether of a misguided nation or a struggling institution. He saw how Samson the Abbot had raised his monastery from a condition of the greatest embarrassment and helplessness to a position of great power and influence."

"So may Englishmen, their eyes being opened to the qualities of their great men, set the heroic element in command and precedence wherever wise organization is required, and thus escape from the dangers which threaten to engulf the social fabric." Carlyle prized Jocelin's memoirs very highly. They amused him with their harmless gossip, but he recognised the transparent truth of the picture they presented of a noble, heroic man, and of a real earnest, God-fearing life clustering round the central figure.†

---

* "Memorials of St. Edmund's Abbey" (Rolls Series), edited by Thomas Arnold.

† So impressed was Carlyle with the "reality of the monk's religion, so transparently mirrored in the chronicle of Jocelin," that he writes: " Our religion—that is, in St. Edmund's Monastery—is not yet a horrible, restless doubt, but a great,

Not a little interest is added to this curious and vivid picture of cloister life when we remember the house from which it came.    The monastery of St. Edmundsbury occupies among the many hundred religious houses which flourished in the days of Cœur de Lion a very distinguished place indeed. It was no recent foundation when Jocelin wrote, owing its existence simply to Norman munificence or Norman penitence.    It belonged to Anglo-Saxon story.    The Normans, it is true, had enriched it and beautified it.    But it was older than the conquerors.    Its patron saint was an Anglo-Saxon king of East Anglia, a realm roughly including our present Eastern Counties, who lived a few years before the great Alfred.    His life has become, it is true, " a poetic rag, a religious mythus," but enough is certainly known about him to construct on a fairly secure basis an historical story of a very noble and brave man who in his lifetime secured the love and devotion of his subjects.

In the Danish conquest of England, Edmund's dominion was specially exposed to the attacks of the sea-kings, two of whom—Hinguar and Hubba—defeated his army with great slaughter at Seven Hills, near Thetford, and shortly after this decisive battle captured King Edmund at Hoxne.    The Pagan victors offered him his life on condition of his renouncing the Christian faith.    Edmund refused, and was bound to a tree, cruelly beaten with clubs, and then shot at with arrows, and subsequently decapitated.[*]

At this point the legendary history which for so many centuries has surrounded the body of King Edmund begins.

heaven-high unquestionability, encompassing, interpenetrating the whole of life. Imperfect as we (the monks of St. Edmund's) may be, we are here with our litanies, our shaven crowns, vows of poverty, to testify incessantly and indisputably to every heart that this earthly life and its riches are not intrinsically a reality at all, but are a shadow of realities, eternal, infinite.    This with our poor litanies we testify."—" Past and Present: *The Ancient Monk*."

  [*] St. Edmund's oak in Hoxne wood was from time immemorial pointed out as the site of the saintly king's martyrdom, and when in September, 1848, this

From a photograph.]                                    [By W. P. Glaisby, York.

**S. EDMUND.**

KING AND MARTYR.

" Heren blys to his mede,
Hem latt have for bys gud dede."

*(From the mural painting in Pickering Church, circa 1450 A.D.)*

The pierced and mangled body of the king was found by
a few of his devoted servants, and reverently buried. But
the head was missing. After forty days' search (some
versions of the story speak of a longer period) the head was

venerable relic of a remote past fell down there was found imbedded deeply in the
ancient trunk an iron cusp which is believed to be one of the actual arrow-blades
shot by the Danes at the king bound to this very tree.—*Journal of the British
Archæological Association,* March, 1865.

Seal of the Abbey of St. Edmundsbury.   In the middle of the seal are two angels carrying the soul of St. Edmund to heaven; at the bottom of the seal is a soldier, represented as having cut off the king's head, which a wolf is guarding.

*(From a fragment appendant to Surrender of Abbey, in the Augmentation Office.)*

found in the woods of Eglesdon safely guarded by an enormous wolf,* which at once quietly yielded up its sacred charge.
It was then reverently placed in the coffin with the body,
with which it immediately united, so that nothing was visible
but a thin line like a purple thread.   The body was found
perfectly undecayed.   For thirty-three years it lay undisturbed in a small wooden church at Hoxne.

Round this little wooden church gathered stories of
miracles of healing worked at the grave of the loved king,
so in A.D. 903 it was determined to erect a large wooden
basilica at the neighbouring town of Beotricsworth, and to lay
there the wonder-working corpse in a shrine.   This basilica
was built of the trunks of large trees sawn lengthways in the

* The wolf guarding the martyr's head has always been represented in the
seal of the abbey arms.

middle, and reared up with one end fixed in the ground with the bark outermost. A few priests and deacons undertook the care of the sacred remains. The fame of the martyr's tomb grew. King Athelstan formed a college of secular canons, to whom the duty of watching over the shrine was entrusted. One of these, Ailwyn by name, became distinguished for his extraordinary devotion to the blessed remains.

The story relates how this Ailwyn became a Benedictine monk, and at his suggestion the charge of the shrine was vested in the order to which Ailwyn belonged. This devoted guardian was in the habit—says one of the chroniclers—of pouring water on the uncorrupt members of the holy body, composing the hair of the head with a comb ; if any hair came off, he carefully kept it as a relic in a box.* In A.D. 1010 Ailwyn brought his sacred charge to London for fear of any harm happening to it from Danish invaders, who were again infesting the Eastern Counties. It remained in London some three years. Some miraculous incidents during its stay in the great city invested the precious relic with ever-increasing fame. Ailwyn resisted the prayer of the Bishop of London who wished to keep the miracle-working body,† and St. Edmund was brought back again to the wooden basilica at the little township of Beotricsworth, the name of which was changed to St. Edmundsbury, for now the fame of the martyr's body and its supposed power attracted many pilgrims, and a considerable town by degrees grew round the wooden basilica which served as the home of the shrine. Already in the reign of Edmund, son of Edward the Elder, A.D. 945, a royal charter and considerable estates, by way of endowment, had been granted to the martyr's shrine and its keepers. The reign of Sweyn the Dane was, however, hostile to the growing " foundation."

* The box and the hair were found by the Commissioners of Henry VIII. in the sixteenth century.

† The Church of St. Edmund, king and martyr, in the City, still preserves the memory of the temporary sojourn of his body in London.

King Sweyn seems to have imposed a grievous tribute on the Eastern Counties, and the lands of the shrine were not exempted. The king listened to the prayer of the servants of St. Edmund that the heavy tax might be remitted, and for a reply mocked at the saint, and threatened to burn the church and town if the tax were not at once paid.

But King Sweyn died, the common report said by the visitation of God and his outraged servant St. Edmund. One of King Sweyn's attendants related the strange story to the monk Ailwyn. It was in the royal camp at Gainsborough, in the evening; the king had gone to bed free from care and happy, suspecting no evil, and when the noise of the royal household had ceased, suddenly there stood before Sweyn, who was still awake, an unknown soldier of wonderful beauty, arrayed in flashing armour, who, calling the king by his name, said: "Dost thou wish, O king, to have the tribute from St. Edmund's land? Arise and take it."

The king arose, and sat up in his bed, but presently, upon seeing the flashing armour, he began to cry terribly. The soldier stabbed him with his lance; the household was awakened by his cries, and running in, found the king besmeared with his own blood, gasping out his life.*

Canute, on succeeding to the whole kingdom, determined to propitiate the formidable saint. He renewed the old charter of King Edmund, vastly enlarging its privileges, and in addition endowing the religious house which had the guardianship of the holy body with so many possessions, that from that time it was looked upon as one of the richest communities in England. He also rebuilt the basilica in the form of a stately church, laying his crown upon St. Edmund's tomb. King Hardicanute paid similar court to the now famous shrine and monastery. Edward the Confessor fre-

* So Richard of Cirencester and William of Malmesbury. Ordericus Vitalis and Hoveden relate the same story with slightly varying details.

quently visited the monks of St. Edmund's, and loved to worship at the altar of the martyr-king whom he called his cousin. The year before his death (A.D. 1065) the Confessor caused his physician, the monk Baldwin of St. Denis (Paris), to be elected abbot of the great monastery.

# CHAPTER II.

## THE BUILDING OF THE ABBEY—A NOTABLE BROTHER.

BALDWIN was the trusted friend, as it happened, of the Norman conqueror William. So the house of St. Edmund and its possessions, in all the bitter troubles which followed the battle of Hastings, remained unharmed, growing indeed year by year in importance and wealth.

Baldwin the physician was a wise and able man, famous even among the great ecclesiastics of that stirring age. It was Baldwin who resisted Herfast, the bishop who wished to live at Bury St. Edmunds, and to make the church which Canute had built over the martyr's tomb the cathedral of his far-reaching East Anglian diocese. But this would have closed the story of the great monastery for ever. Abbot Baldwin went to Rome, and from Pope Alexander II. received a brief of privilege, which made St. Edmund's house independent of episcopal control, and placed it under the special protection* of the Roman pontiff. The Pope gave him a pastoral staff, and thus raised him in rank above other abbots, and enriched his church with the famous porphyry

---

* So great and marked was the favour ever shown by Rome to this house, that some sixty bulls were granted by succeeding Popes to confirm and enlarge its rights and privileges.

altar, on which mass was to be celebrated, though the whole kingdom around lay under an interdict. In addition to all these spiritual privileges the Norman kings in succession, among many marks of royal favour, confirmed the charter of the Confessor given to Baldwin, allowing the abbot to coin money, with all the rights of a royal mint.

Abbot Baldwin was a true Norman ecclesiastic of the highest type, and the spirit which inspired so many of the spiritual chieftains of that strange, mighty race, which in the eleventh century looked to William the Conqueror as their lord, rested also upon the physician-abbot of St. Edmund's. Men like Baldwin were persuaded that

their Master's religion would win a greater hold upon
the human soul if they could celebrate the mysteries of
the Christian faith and teach their holy doctrines in
abbeys, minsters, and cathedrals, which, from their vast
size, their gorgeous decorations and sacred symbolism,
would at once inspire awe and stimulate enthusiasm.   They
believed that from these magnificent and stately centres
a new work of conversion would issue.   They felt that
the stately abbey and the noble cathedral would serve
to attract men and lavish offerings to be used in the
service of the King of kings.   They chose the moment well.
There never was a time before or since in England like the
years which immediately followed the Norman Conquest for
the carrying out of their gigantic works.

And of all the splendid houses of God which this great
church-building age saw designed, and to a certain measure
completed, the abbey of St. Edmund, the abbey of Baldwin
the physician to the Confessor and the Conqueror, was perhaps the grandest.*   From the poor sad ruins with us now,
we can still accurately measure the amazing magnitude of
its dimensions; as a Norman edifice it far surpassed in size
every other church or cathedral in the kingdom of that era.†
An eye-witness ‡ speaks of its vaulting, its pillars, its marbles
as all being on the noblest scale; never was a more beautiful and magnificent minster seen than the lordly abbey of
the Eastern Counties which rose so proudly over the shrine of
the East Saxon Edmund in the days of Rufus.   At the close
of the eleventh century the abbey was a favourite place of
sepulture.   Here were brought from their original resting-

* The abbey was almost entirely rebuilt by Baldwin. It was, of course,
not completed in his time.

† *Journal of the British Archæological Association*, March, 1865, " Bury
St. Edmunds Abbey," by Gordon M. Hills (paper 1).

‡ Herman, the archdeacon, who wrote his " *De Miraculis S. Edmundi*" at
the close of the eleventh century.—Rolls Series, " Memorials of St. Edmund's
Abbey."   1890.

places the remains of several of the East Anglian kings ; here, too, were laid, among other famous personages, the bodies of Alan, Earl of Bretagne, son-in-law of the Conqueror ; Alan Rufus, Earl of Richmond, who commanded the rear-guard at Hastings ; Constance, Countess of Bretagne, the Conqueror's second daughter, and others.

The conventual buildings around this stupendous abbey were in no respect unworthy of their glorious centre. They were on a scale of magnitude not surpassed in England. One peculiar feature was the stately group of seven or perhaps eight churches or chapels in the cemetery which partly surrounded the abbey, two if not more of these being of great size and magnificence. The importance of this, perhaps the greatest of the English Benedictine abbeys of the early Middle Ages, was universally recognised. Nearly every chronicler between the eleventh and fifteenth centuries found occasion to refer to it, beginning with the Saxon Chronicle and Asser's "Life of Alfred" in the eleventh century, and ending with Walsingham, who wrote in the fifteenth. Some fourteen well-known chroniclers might be quoted who refer to important matters connected with the great house.

Such was the home of prayer under whose broad shadow the monks of St. Edmund's lived that life in the days of Cœur de Lion and his father, so vividly and charmingly portrayed by one of their number in his unique and homelike picture of the everyday doings and sayings of his brother monks.

The Memoirs of Jocelin open somewhat abruptly.*

The writer was a young monk just out of his novitiate, and his earliest impressions of this great house were, that

* The Chronicle of Jocelin, a monk of St. Edmund's, here referred to, embraces the period from 1173 A.D. to 1202 A.D. It is written in "Monk-Latin," and was first printed from a MS. in the Harleian Collection by the Camden Society in 1840. The Camden edition is a quarto, and the text occupies 103 pages. Here a few extracts only have been taken from the chronicle, extracts which especially throw light upon the inner life of a great monastery of the twelfth century.

while there was much earnest religion and real devotion among his brethren, there prevailed at the same time a sad laxity of discipline and an utter disregard of finance; the great officers of the monastery—the priors, sacrist, cellarer, and others—did what they liked. The vast revenues of St. Edmund's were grievously wasted; the farms, manor-houses, and even the buildings of the monks and abbot were in sad want of repair, and ready money was always lacking, and large sums were constantly borrowed from Jewish usurers at a ruinous rate of interest (sixty per cent. !).

Jocelin said all this was owing to the weakness of the Lord Abbot—"a pious and kind man was Abbot Hugh (once prior of Westminster), a good and religious monk," but now an old man half blind and tormented with rheumatism. He had been abbot some twenty-three years, and in his old age was sadly influenced by flatterers, who deceived him as to the true state of affairs in the monastery.

Fortunately for St. Edmund's, Abbot Hugh wished to pray at the shrine of St. Thomas of Canterbury. On the journey his horse stumbled, and the poor old man was mortally hurt, and only returned to his beautiful home to die. A sad picture of the discipline of the abbey we have here, for Jocelin tells us, no sooner was Hugh dead, than his servants plundered everything in his house that they could carry away, and not a single article of a penny's worth was left that could be distributed to the poor for his soul's sake.

A similar scene of ingratitude and sordid greed, Ordericus Vitalis tells us, was witnessed when William the Conqueror breathed his last at St. Gervais, on the hill by Rouen.

Now who was to be abbot of the famous foundation ? It was no small prize. The Dominus Abbas of St. Edmund's was a mighty man in the State as well as in the Church. Fifty knights and their dependants followed his banner. The income of the house has been calculated at £300,000

of our money, or even more.
If the abbot was an able prelate he sat as a royal coun-
cillor in all important public matters.

There was at this time on the throne a very powerful
and masterful king, Henry II. Would he let the monks
elect one of their own body, or would he force some stranger
to them, into the abbot's chair? Fortunately for the house
at this juncture a foreign ecclesiastic of high rank, well
known to the king, the Archbishop of Drontheim, in Norway,
who had been driven by state intrigues from his see, was the
guest of England.

For some months after Hugh's death the archbishop
resided in the monastery of St. Edmund, and reported well
to Henry II. of the piety and learning of the house. Of
their money difficulties and wasteful administration probably

H

the foreign archbishop knew nothing, so after a longish interregnum of over a year, the king commanded the prior and twelve representative monks to appear before him and make choice of an abbot. One of the most curious bits of Jocelin's memoirs describes the monks' gossipy talk, at recreation and at other seasons when talk was permissible, about their favourite chiefs and officers, dwelling on the special qualifications of the more prominent brothers for the high office then vacant.

One would say of another, " That brother is a good monk ; he is well acquainted with the rule and discipline of the Church, and though he may not be as perfect a philosopher as others, he is well able to be an abbot. Was not Abbot Ording* an illiterate man ? yet he was a good abbot, and governed the house wisely."

Then another would answer, " How may this be ? Can an unlearned man preach a sermon in chapter to us, or to the people on Sunday ? Far be it that a dumb statue should be set up in the church of St. Edmund, where many learned and studious men are known to be."

Another would be heard to say, " That brother is a good clerk, eloquent and careful, strict in rule, he hath well loved the house; he is worthy to be made an abbot." He would be answered, " From good clerks, O Lord, deliver us, as from lawyer-like brothers."†

One monk would say, " That brother is a good steward, we see it from the way he has filled his office ; see how many thorough repairs he has carried out; he is too by no means deficient in wit, though it is true too much learning hath not made him mad." But his friend would reply to these

---

* A well-known and popular prior, and subsequently abbot some years before 1156.

† This was a side hit at Samson the sub-sacrist who became abbot, but who by his zeal and energy had made a certain number of enemies.

praises: "Surely God would never have a man for an abbot who can neither read, write, nor chant."

Another would answer then, "There is a brother who is a kind man, amiable, peace-loving, open-hearted, and generous, learned too and eloquent, beloved by many indoors as well as out; such a man might by God's leave become abbot to the great honour of the Church." But his friend would ironically paint another view of this popular character: "It would be surely an honour to the Church to have an abbot over-nice in his eating and drinking, one who thinks it a virtue to sleep long, who spends much and gets little, who sleeps while others watch, who cares nothing for the debts * which grow day by day—a man cherishing and fostering flatterers and liars—from such a prelate, defend us, O Lord!"

One monk thus spoke of a brother: "That man is wiser than all of us put together, both in worldly and Church matters, a man of lofty counsel, strict in rule, eloquent and learned; would not he be a good prelate?" "Yes," said his friend, "if only his reputation were good; but his character is doubtful; he certainly seems wise, meek and humble in chapter, devoted in church, strict in the cloister, but it is all outward show with him! What if he do excel in any office, he is too scornful, lightly esteems monks, is closely intimate with secular persons."

Again a certain monk who seemed in his own eye very wise, said, "May the Lord bestow on us a simple and foolish shepherd, so that it may be most needful for Him to care for us."

The novices said, "Infirm old men were by no means fit to govern a convent." Thus many persons said many things.

---

* The monk here was evidently alluding to some favourite officers of the late abbot Hugh, who allowed the affairs of the monastery to get into sad confusion, allowing flatterers to deceive him as to the real state of the house.

Jocelin tells us how he gave his own opinion in these little cloister gatherings. He would not have the choice fall on too good a monk, or an overwise clerk, neither on one too simple or too weak, lest on the one hand he should be over-confident in his own judgment and despise others, or, on the other hand, lest he through weakness should become a by-word to others.

There was in the monastery a certain monk of the name of Samson, a man of good lineage, not quite fifty years old, who had filled several important offices in the house with honour and credit, such as master of the town schools, master of the novices, and latterly sub-sacrist, an "obedience" involving in such a great house onerous and important duties. He was a reserved, thoughtful man, of great business capabilities, a good scholar, and an able preacher, very earnest and devout, but in an unostentatious manner.

This monk was no favourite with the late abbot, for he would never join the band of sycophants who, to serve their own ends, made it their business to hide from the old ailing abbot the disorders which were creeping into the community. Samson would boldly speak his mind in public chapter when he saw things going wrong, and thus made not a few enemies by his plain, honest words. When Hugh died he was collecting funds and materials for building one of the great towers of the church. The wisest of the monks thought highly of their sub-sacrist Samson as one who could and would, if he had the power, restore the relaxed discipline and set in order the disordered finances of the house.

But though he was one of the twelve selected to go to the king, he was evidently not looked on generally as a likely candidate for the abbatical dignity, as he was almost unknown outside the walls of St. Edmund's. The prior and the twelve bore with them a sealed paper for the king in which were the

The Abbey Gate
Bury St. Edmunds

Built *circa* A.D. 1327.

names of three brothers fitted in all respects for the abbacy. These names were secretly selected by six senior monks chosen for that purpose by the whole house. The three names so chosen in solemn privacy were Samson, Hugo, the third prior, and Roger, the cellarer, a great officer in the monastery.

Henry II., who was at Waltham, in Hampshire, received the monks of St. Edmund's very graciously, and desired them to nominate to him three members of their community who seemed to them worthy of the abbacy. The prior and the twelve then withdrew and opened and read aloud their sealed instructions. Jocelin tells us of the surprised faces when the names were read out, and how those brethren who were of higher rank than the three nominated, flushed—*erubuerunt*—(a momentary feeling of surprise and a little jealousy; Jocelin conceals nothing). The king listened and was puzzled. They were quite unknown names to the outside world. "Let them suggest," said Henry, "three more names that he might have a wider choice."

They consulted together: William, the sacrist, a great official but a careless, bad monk, said to the brethren, "Our prior ought to be nominated, because he is our head."

All agreed at once. In the first flush of gratitude for his nomination, the prior, who seems to have been—although of stainless character—a weak man, nominated the sacrist; the third suggested was an old monk, Dennis, a man of blameless life, but possessing no special ability.

They presented these fresh names to King Henry, who marvelled, saying, "These electors have been quick about it; God is with them. But give me," said the king, "yet a wider choice, and suggest to me as well three names of strangers to your house." Rather reluctantly, for they wished to keep the great office to the brethren of St. Edmund's, they nominated three well-known stranger monks from Malmesbury, St. Faith's, and St. Neot's.

The king considered a while, and told them to strike out three from the nine. At once they struck off the three aliens; of the six remaining four were by agreement among themselves withdrawn, and now but two remained as the free choice of the house of St. Edmund's, the prior and Samson. Richard, bishop of Winchester, and Geoffrey, the son of fair Rosamund, the chancellor, stood by the king as counsellors. The venerable old monk Dennis then acted as spokesman for the rest of the brothers, commending the persons of the prior and Samson, saying that each of them was learned, that either was good, but he kept coming back in the corner of his discourse *(in angulo sui sermonis)* to Samson, repeating that he was a man in very truth strict in life, severe in reforming excesses, moreover heedful in secular matters (the wise old monk remembered well the faults of the late abbot), and approved in various offices.

The Bishop of Winchester replied, "We see what you wish to say. Your prior seems to have been somewhat remiss, and that, in fact, you wish to have Samson." "Either of them is good," answered Dennis, "but by God's help we desire to have the best." The Bishop of Winchester then asked them plainly, "Is it your wish to have Samson?" Then it was answered by the majority of the little company of delegates, "We will have Samson."

The king, after a consultation with those about him, said, "You present to me Samson; I know him not. Had you presented to me your prior I should at once have accepted him, because I have known him, and am well acquainted with him; but I will do as you desire me. Take heed to yourselves; by the eyes of God,* if you are acting unworthily, I shall call you to severe account." Then he asked the prior if he assented to the choice. The prior, who had so narrowly missed the great office himself, very generously and nobly said he was well content it should be so, and that Samson was much more worthy of the dignity.

At once the new lord abbot fell down at the king's feet and, kissing them, hastily arose and went towards the altar, saying, "*Miserere mei Deus*," erect, and with an unmoved countenance. The king watched him. "By the eyes of God," said Henry to the ministers of state standing by him,

* These strange adjurations were ever on the lips of the great Norman and Angevin kings. The Conqueror used to swear by the "Splendour of God," Rufus by the "Holy face of Lucca."

"this one that is chosen evidently thinks himself worthy of the abbacy."

The story of Jocelin then goes on to relate how the Bishop of Winchester placed the mitre on Abbot Samson's head and the ring on his finger. He tells too of the stately welcome given by the monks to their brother whom they had chosen for the great office, and relates how a thousand persons were dinner guests on the eventful day of his return.

But more interesting far than the records of all the high feasting is Jocelin's account of the solemn service in the stately abbey, when the new abbot, barefooted, was led up to his throne to implore the blessing of the King of kings on the arduous life-work which lay before him, the monks of the house singing the quaint sweet hymn of Edmund before the shrine of the loved East Anglian king, whose body, still unchanged, beautiful as when he died some three centuries back, was the glory of the great monastery of the Eastern Counties—

MARTYRI ADHUC PALPITANTI
SED CHRISTUM CONFITENTI
JUSSIT HINGUAR* CAPUT AUFERRI;
SICQUE EADMUNDUS MARTYRIUM CONSUMMAVIT,
ET AD DEUM EXULTANS VADIT.

It was a proud and very solemn hour for the poor monk. For this great work had he trained himself unconsciously through many patient, toil-filled years; but it was no rose-leaf couch he found in the stately abbot's chamber, whose crumbling stones we can still gaze on in the garden of the ruins, washed by the little silvery stream of the Lark. In less than ten years care and sorrows had left their stern mark on Abbot Samson; the ruddy beard and the wavy hair we read of in the picture drawn by Jocelin of the earnest master of the novices† had become as white as snow.

* Hinguar was the Viking chief who slew King Edmund.
† The office once held by Samson, in which he probably gained his great reputation.

# CHAPTER III.

## The Great Abbot and his Biographer.

LELAND, the secretary of King Henry VIII., who visited the abbey just before the work of destruction commenced, has left us in his famous "Itinerary" the following glowing description of the great house of our story.

"The sun hath not shone on a town more delightfully situated on a gradual and easy descent, with a small river flowing on the eastern part, or on a monastery more illustrious, whether we consider its wealth, its extent, or its incomparable magnificence; you might indeed say that the monastery itself is a town—so many gates there are, some of them of brass; so many towers, and a church than which none can be more magnificent; . . . the rivulet mentioned above, with an arched bridge thrown over it, glides through the bounds of the monastery."

Of all the splendour which so impressed Leland, there remain only two stately gateways, the one dating back to the days of Beauclerc, the other to the early part of the reign of Edward III., to mark the site of this most magnificent of abbeys. The two grand parish churches, St. James's and St. Mary's—solitary remnants of the seven churches or chapels which once formed a noble and striking group in

I

the abbey cemetery—are still standing. The beautiful
Abbot's Bridge (A.D. 1225), which spans the river Lark, is
also preserved.

Shapeless piles of scarred and disfigured masonry, too
much defaced even to be picturesque, are the sad remains of
the stupendous church and of the vast buildings which surrounded it. These are scattered over several acres of grassy
meadow which gently slopes down to the little river Lark.
The largest portion of the great enclosure of the monastery
has been laid out with some care as a public garden, and girls
and little children play their games, and fill the air with the
music of their child voices, thinking little of the forgotten life,
with its joys and sorrows, with its hopes and tragedies, which
went on for so many hundred years in the garden of the ruins.

In one spot the broken piles of massive masonry are more
huge, rise to a far greater height, and are beautiful with that

strange weird beauty which a vast and even shapeless ruin alone possesses. The broken, formless stones here are clothed with many-coloured memories—memories which can never die. These great piles represent the abbey church of St. Edmund, which was vaster than most of our great cathedrals, and once beautiful as a dream, with its forest of sculptured columns, its fretted roof gleaming with gold and colour, its pictured walls, its rich pavements, its dim-lit altars, its jewelled shrines — all designed by master-builders and cunning artists, whose splendid works men nowadays strive to copy rather than to excel.

But besides these huge, shapeless fragments, marking roughly the site of the abbey tower and transept, there is yet another relic, perhaps more sad. The stranger—as he stands in the old abbey cemetery— looks upon a long line of grey rubble of enormous thickness and strength, into which two considerable

Erected *circa* A.D. 1120.

dwelling-houses and some public offices have been crowded; he sees the remains of mighty arches curiously filled with doors and windows, with wooden roofs grotesquely piled above, crowning this strange creation of modern times.

This long line of grey rubble, stretching nearly two hundred and fifty feet, was the core of the lower part of the great west front of the abbey. It is thirty to fifty feet in height. Well-nigh every piece of cut stone long ago was stripped away from the flint rubble by heedless spoilers, and the almost imperishable core, of enormous thickness, has been utilised in this singular way for modern dwelling-houses.

This scarred and defaced ruin, we can still see, contains three arches, smaller than those of the west front of Peterborough but larger than the corresponding features at Lincoln Cathedral. These originally formed a front to the nave and its north and south aisles. Each aisle, the remains show us, was flanked by a chapel, the west end of which formed an extension to the west end of the great church. These were again outflanked by two octagon towers, giving to the west end of the abbey a vastness of dimension with which no church in England, so far as is known, could have competed.

Such is the present aspect of the once stately monastery in which Jocelin, the author of the graceful gossiping story of Abbot Samson, lived and prayed and worked, and—happily for us—wrote.

Jocelin's memoirs, as we possess them, stretch over about twenty years of Abbot Samson's reign. During six of these years he was attached, by his office of chaplain, very closely to the abbot; at other periods of his long monastic life Jocelin held different important and responsible offices in the great house of St. Edmund's, such as almoner, guest-master, &c. For several years after his installation, Abbot Samson's principal troubles were connected with his setting in order the financial matters of the community.

He was completely successful. The rule here of the late abbot had been, as we have seen, very lax, and it was four years before the enormous debt to Jewish usurers was all paid off. "My heart," he was heard constantly to say, "will never rest until I know myself to be out of debt." One of the great officers, William, the sacrist, whom we

heard of at the visit of the monks to the court of Henry II., was one of the chief offenders in the careless administration of the property of the monastery. Samson soon deposed this official, who was guilty of various excesses besides money-recklessness—"wine-bibbing, and certain other acts not to be named."

"Behold," the abbot said, on one occasion, when explaining the reason of his extreme severity to the assembled chapter, "the results of the mismanagement of the sacrist—see the multitude of securities signed with his official seal—how he has pledged the property of the community, silver cups, dalmatics, censers of silver, books ornamented with gold." The house of this careless, loose-living, but perhaps popular officer, which was in the garden, the abbot caused, as a terrible example, to be levelled with the ground—"so that within the year, upon the spot where a noble building had stood, we saw beans growing, and where casks of wine had been placed we saw nettles flourishing."

The picture of one of the earnest thirteenth-century abbots gives us the idea of a life crowded with work, much of it difficult and even painful. It was not only over his great house and its vast property and enormous responsibilities that he had to watch; many state and public cares fell also to his lot.

Constant encroachment on the part of the king, ever needy and impecunious, had to be resisted; high-handed, and often vicious, proceedings on the part of the Norman barons in his part of England had to be guarded against. These great ecclesiastical functionaries were, in those days, one of the bulwarks of the people against grinding tyranny and selfish oppression.

Our abbot was a man of considerable learning, and in earlier days he had been master of the town schools. After his elevation we hear of his preaching eloquently in three languages. Among his many works in his beautiful abbey we read of a pulpit he erected, one of its notable ornaments, and how from this pulpit he was in the habit of preaching to the people in their homely Norfolk dialect.

His chaplain gives us a picture of his hero in the days when he was a plain monk, and paints him as a strong, stout-made man of seven-and-forty, erect as a pillar, with bushy eyebrows, wavy hair, and a long-flowing ruddy beard very slightly streaked with grey, with piercing eyes looking out of a grave, massive face. After wearing for ten years the abbot's mitre he was as white as snow. He was never an ascetic, but was ever utterly careless of what he ate or drank.

His chaplain slept near him in the abbot's lodge. One night Jocelin relates how, after one of the night services, he heard his lord wakeful, and sighing heavily. He asked him in the morning the cause. The abbot said to him, "'No wonder; thou hast partaken of my good things, in meat, and drink, and riding abroad, and such like ; thou needst not care much about the ruling of the abbey, and household of the saints, all the arduous cares which harass me, and make my spirit to groan and be very heavy and sad.' 'God deliver me,' I replied, 'from such crushing cares as these.'

" At another time I heard the lord abbot say, 'If I could only have foreseen what an awful charge it had been to govern the abbey, I would have chosen rather to be master of the almonry and of the doles to the poor, or, better still, to be keeper of the books than lord abbot.' " "Night and day," says Jocelin, "for six years I was ever with him, and had the chance of knowing thoroughly the goodness of his life, and all about his wise rule."

His faithful chronicler, among a number of petty details of work, alludes to the abbot's constant care of the abbey and the monastic buildings; how, when even he was sub-sacrist, he watched over the repairs of the great church, bestowing infinite pains on the collecting of money and materials for these necessary but unnoticed works. As abbot he erected over the vast abbey estates an infinite number of useful and not a few religious edifices, such as churches, hospitals, and schools ; but his greatest building work seems to have been the noble tower of St. Edmund's, and we shall see presently how he beautified and adorned the shrine of his patron saint, the object of so many devout pilgrimages.

Far on in the chronicle we come to a specially interesting memorandum of Jocelin, which he wrote evidently in almost middle life, long after he had ceased to be the abbot's chaplain. It was penned in the year 1198.

A quarter of a century had passed since the young novice of St. Edmund's had taken the solemn life-long vows of a Benedictine monk. Jocelin, now middle-aged, had become

*A Fragment in the Abbey Garden.*

the hospitaler or guest-master.  After all these years he
still writes of his dear master Samson with his old enthusiasm,
when he describes in his vivid, picturesque words what his
well-beloved abbot had done within the walls of the noble
monastery.

   " And now the long-hoped-for time, the long-wished-for
day has arrived, whereof I write not but with great joy,
myself having the care of the guests.  So at the command
of the abbot, the court resounds with spades and masons'
tools for pulling down the guest-house, and now it is almost
down—of the rebuilding let the Most High take thought.
. . .  The chapels of St. Andrew, and St. Katherine, and
St. Faith are newly roofed with lead ; many restorations are
made inside and outside the church.  If you will not believe,
open your eyes and see.  By our abbot too was built our
stone almonry—it was of wood before, and had become
ruinous.  Walter, the physician, one of us, gave for these
works much of what he had gained by his practice of physic."

Cœur de Lion's captivity seems to have seriously affected the monastery of St. Edmund ; the guest-master sadly misses many costly and beautiful ornaments of the abbey and the shrine. The precious silver table of the high altar was gone—it had been sold to help to pay the ransom of King Richard—and many other treasured ornaments had been parted with for the same object. The wise abbot would not replace these, because, he said, they would probably have to be sold again for some state necessity, so he turned his attention to adorning the shrine of the glorious martyr Edmund. "And now the plates of gold and silver for the shrine's crest"—wrote Jocelin—"resound between the hammer and anvil. No one would dare to ask for these, even for the king's ransom."

Men like Samson were devotedly loyal, stern though he was in his refusal to yield to the king, when Richard required what was unjust at his hands. Cœur de Lion had no subject in all his broad dominions more chivalrously devoted to him than the noble abbot of our story. When the king was a captive in Germany, no one exactly knowing where the foul treachery of his brother crusader, the Duke of Austria, had imprisoned him, Abbot Samson from his place in Parliament started up before all the peers, and offered to go in search of his master; and surely enough he went to find him, taking rich gifts with him for Richard. No one too in England was more determined in resisting the king's traitorous brother, John Lackland, who wished to take advantage of his gallant brother's enforced absence.

But he knew when to resist unlawful tyranny. One well-known incident Jocelin relates at considerable length. When Cœur de Lion wished to give away a ward of Abbot Samson, a child heiress, the little daughter of the dead Adam de Cokefield, to one of his needy courtiers, Samson repeatedly refused, and would not give the richly-dowered

K

girl up to the king's messengers. "Tell the king," I said,
"let the Most High look to it—*videat Altissimus.*" When
the royal anger at the abbot's message had abated, as so
often was the case with this impulsive but generous sovereign,
he repented himself, and honoured the sturdy English abbot
who preferred offending the king of England to the King of
kings. Richard, on this occasion, sent Abbot Samson, as a
mark of his friendship, a ring of great price which Pope
Innocent III. had given him.

Our abbot, though, was something more than an un-
wearied head of a great house, more than a prudent
administrator of many farm-lands, more than a wise royal
counsellor, or even than a devotedly loyal friend to his king,
more than a thoughtful and stainless steward of great possessions. Beneath all these splendid and useful qualities,
there was in the monk's heart the deepest reverence for
things unseen, the most fervid love for his Master in
heaven.

Abbot Samson was a religious man, pious in the truest,
deepest sense. We wonder now at the strange passion
which, in the eleventh and following centuries, moved men to
try and rescue the Holy City and the sacred places out of
the hands of unbelievers; we marvel at the burning zeal
which induced men to give up home and hearth, and all
that makes life pleasant and desirable, in the hope of driving
out the infidel from the land which the feet of the Redeemer
had pressed during His earthly pilgrimage. The Redeemer is
still as precious to us as in those far-back days—perhaps
more precious, but we care little for the desolate cities and
the sad hills and valleys of the Holy Land.

Our zeal and fervour for the Lord now take a very different course. But when Cœur de Lion lived, among western
peoples no earthly enterprise was so noble, no ointment
could be poured upon the Redeemer's feet so precious, as the

crusader's strange service. In most cases taking the cross involved the sternest sacrifice of self—life and home were risked.

When King Henry II. had taken the cross, and had, as Jocelin writes, "come to us for the sake of paying his devotions," Abbot Samson, though he was no soldier, determined to leave his glorious abbey and his fair home, and as a plain fighting man strike in that far-away, deadly land a blow in defence of his dear Lord's Holy City. " The abbot privily made for himself a crusader's habit of linen cloth, and, holding in one hand a cross and a needle and thread, he requested permission from the king to fasten it on his shoulder, but the king denied him this favour." The Bishop of Norwich was going too as a crusader, and the king deemed it unsafe for the abbot of St. Edmund's to be out of the Eastern Counties at the same time as the bishop.

But Abbot Samson—though at the bidding of his king he gave up the perilous expedition—never in the midst of his many cares

*Seal of Abbot Samson.*

*(From an Instrument in the Archives of Canterbury Cathedral, dated Nov. 6, A.D. 1200.)*

allowed Jerusalem to be away from his thoughts. And when he heard that the Holy City was retaken by the Pagan armies, his faithful chronicler tells us how the abbot, still wearing outwardly the insignia of his high rank, put on (for ever) under-garments of horsehair and a horsehair shirt, and while still directing that flesh and flesh meats should, as heretofore, be placed on his table for the sake of the alms dish (the poor received these dishes after the abbot had dined), for ever after abstained from these things. Men knew not of this mortification, of this stern abstinence—only God.

" Shall Samson Abbas take pleasure when Christ's tomb is in the hands of the infidel ? Samson in pain of body shall be daily reminded of it, daily be admonished to grieve for it." " It was not a dilettantism this of our Abbot. It was a reality, and it is one. The garment only of it is dead, the essence of it lives through all time and eternity ! " Our great historic writer especially admires, with a strong ungrudging admiration, our monk's comparative silence as to his religion, " the healthiest sign of him and of it—Abbot Samson, all along a busy, working man, as all men are bound to be ; his religion, his worship was like his daily bread to him ; which he did not take the trouble to talk much about, which he merely ate at stated intervals, and lived and did his work upon. This is Abbot Samson's Catholicism of the twelfth century."*

Jocelin, the author of the chronicle which gives us this vivid picture of an interior of a great twelfth-century monastery—a picture which we feel is transparently true—is described by a brother monkish writer as " a man excellently religious, powerful in speech and work." He ends his memoir abruptly at the beginning of the year 1202 ; we know not what put so sudden a close to his charming story. Involuntarily we turn the page of the chronicle over, but there is no more ! " Our real phantasmagory of St. Edmundsbury plunges into the bosom of the twelfth century again, and all is over. Monks, abbot, hero-worship, Cœur de Lion, St. Edmund's shrine, vanish like Mirza's vision ; and there is nothing left

* Carlyle, " Past and Present : *The Ancient Monk*," chap. xv.

but a mutilated black ruin amid green botanic expanse, and oxen, sheep, and dilettanti pasturing in their places."*

Abbot Samson lived ten years after the last date in Jocelin's record. An unknown monk† thus writes of him : "On the 30th December (1212 A.D.) at St. Edmund's, died Samson of pious memory, the venerable abbot of that place, who, after he had prosperously ruled for thirty years the abbey committed to him, and had freed it from a load of debt, had enriched it with privileges, liberties, possessions, and spacious buildings, and had restored the worship of the church both within and without in the most ample manner, bidding his last farewell to his sons, by whom the blessed man deserved to be blest for evermore, while they were all standing by,‡ and gazing with awe at a death which was a cause for admiration not for regret (*non miserabilem sed mirabilem*), in the fourth year of the Interdict (of King John's reign) rested in peace."

* Carlyle, " Past and Present : *The Ancient Monk,*" chap. xvi.

† See Chronicle in Harl. 447, quoted by Mr. Arnold ; " Memorials of St. Edmund's Abbey," Rolls Series, intro., liii.

‡ Compare the account of the usual scene of the death of a monk in the story of the death-scene of Hugh of Lincoln.

# CHAPTER IV.

## THE SHRINE OF ST. EDMUND AND WHAT IT CONTAINED.

IT is strange that the visible centre of this glorious group of prayer-homes—the abbey and the seven churches and chapels grouped round it, which almost from the cradle to the grave sheltered, educated, watched over so many generations of Englishmen, who in their day did not a little towards the making of our England—was a little gilded jewelled shrine which held the poor remains of a long-dead hero-king.

Hero-worship, saint-worship, martyr-worship, has always played, will always play, a large part in the life-story of true men and loving women. It is not of course the highest ideal of worship, but very many religious men in all ages tell us it helps them to the sublimer worship, assists them in forming loftier, nobler conceptions of the Unseen. However, in such a simple historical study as this, we must accept and relate truly what we find, hardly attempting to explain or excuse what perhaps seems to us regrettable superstition, certainly never throwing, with our puny strength, stones at the memory of great and good men who, after their light, lived noble lives, even if we fail to grasp some of the motives of their conduct.

*The Shrine of St. Edmund.*

The story of the honoured body of King Edmund in the golden shrine of the great abbey is a striking one. How it began we have already told; its progress is thus described.

" The wooden chapel where the Saint-king lay has become a stone Temple. Stately masonries begirdle it far and wide. Regimented companies of men devote themselves in every generation to meditate here on man's Nobleness and Awfulness, and celebrate and show forth the same as best they can, thinking they will do it better here in the presence of God the Maker and of the so awful and noble made by him. In one word, St. Edmund's body has raised a monastery round it." *

All sorts and conditions of men, besides the vowed monks, loved to come and pray to God by the tomb of the saint. They said they could think better, pray better, there for

* Carlyle.

home and hearth and wife and child. They dreamed in their trustful, childish way St. Edmund could help them,* and so they prayed more earnestly in that stately choir by the shrine than in castle or cottage.

The unvarying tradition related that the body of the martyred king underwent no corruption ; there was also a belief that the severed head became united with the body. As on several well-authenticated occasions the coffin or *loculus* was opened and the body seen, the probable explanation of the so-called "miracle of incorruption" is that the body was skilfully embalmed. The second prodigy, the uniting of the severed head with the trunk, seems less clearly authenticated. Abbot Samson is said by Jocelin "to have taken the head in his hands" when the *loculus* was opened, which act might certainly give a very different interpretation to the ordinary legend.

In the early Middle Ages there were four distinct recorded identifications of the body. The first of these was in A.D. 925 by Theodred, bishop of Elmham (Eastern Counties), who was afterwards translated to London in the reign of Athelstan. We read how Theodred, after a three days' fast, opened the coffin and removed the blood-stained clothes from the body, which, after washing, he re-clothed.

The second was by the monk Aylwin, originally one of the College of Secular Canons of St. Edmund's, subsequently a Benedictine monk and bishop of Elmham. Aylwin seems to have been in charge of the saint's body, and for years to

---

* Compare the words of an ancient antiphon which used to be sung in the abbey on his feast day—

> Ave, rex gentis Anglorum,
> Miles Regis angelorum,
> O Edmunde flos militum,
> Velut rosa, velut lilium,
> Funde preces ad Dominum
> Pro salute fidelium.

The supposition was simply that Edmund should pray for them to God.

have shown extraordinary devotion to the glorified Edmund.
Men say how he would frequently spend the night in prayer
at the shrine, and that oftentimes the saint would commune
with him. Lydgate, who compiled in the reign of Henry VI·
a metrical life of the martyr-king, wrote of this monk Aylwin
that, so great was his perfection, many a time the Saint
and he—

> " Spak togiþre mouth to mouth
> Touchynge hih' thynges off contemplacioun,
> Expert ful ofte, be rebelacioun
> Off hebenly thynges, to speke in woordes fewe,
> Þe gostly secretys which God lyst to hym shewe."*

This Aylwin's custom was at some " fitt times " to open his
sepulchre, to wash the sacred body, and reverently to comb
the hair. This identification (apparently often repeated) took
place in A.D. 990 and following years.

The third was in the time of the Confessor, A.D. 1050,
under the direction of Leofstan, the second Benedictine abbot.
The body then was found to be perfect, apparently asleep,
and so beautiful as to suggest the idea of one risen from the
dead. An ineffable sweet odour was diffused through the
great church and cloisters, quite different to the odour of
incense. The blood-stained clothes were still in the *loculus.*

Abbot Leofstan, desirous of testing the current miracle—
we read—took the head of Edmund between his hands and
pulled it towards him—and the whole body followed. The
abbot immediately replaced the remains, but found his hands
paralysed and distorted. This grave result of his faithless
experiment was, so runs the story, the merciful answer to his
prayer that he might be punished for his incredulity in this
life, not in the next.

The fourth identification was in A.D. 1198 by Abbot
Samson, and it is told by Jocelin at great length. It is one of
the most charming pieces of his chronicle—full of vivid and

* MS. Harl., 2278, fol. 101—v.

L

picturesque details. The writer, Jocelin, had years before ceased to be the abbot's chaplain, and was at this time (A.D. 1198) one of the chief officers of the monastery, the guest-master, and he bemoans his absence when the *loculus* was opened—"I, alas, was not present."

The abbot had for some time determined that the shrine which held the body of St. Edmund should be enriched and beautified. An accidental fire, kindled through the carelessness of some sleepy monks, whose duty it was to watch near the holy body in the night hours, seriously damaged some of the stonework belonging to the high altar, in the neighbourhood of which the *loculus*, with its sacred contents, was placed. This determined the abbot to press on the work.

Jocelin tells us how, the festival of St. Edmund now being near, the new marble blocks—intended to serve as a base for the shrine—were polished, and everything was made ready to raise the shrine upon them. A three days' fast was ordered. After the fast, in the night, coming in to matins, the monks found the great shrine raised on the altar—where it was to rest until the masons' work was completed—but still empty. It was adorned with white doe-skins fastened to the wood with silver nails. The *loculus* with the sacred body was below in its old place by a column of the church. Later in the day the abbot and certain with him, clothed in their albs, proceeded to uncover the sacred chest.

First there was an outer cloth of linen, overwrapping the coffin, within that was a silken cloth, then two more linen wrappers, and so at last the coffin was uncovered standing on wood, that the bottom might not be rubbed by the stone. An angel of gold (St. Michael) about a foot long was fastened outside. The *loculus* was of wood with iron rings —as there used to be on the Danish coffin (*in cistâ Norensi*).

"Some of us who were called by the abbot" (Jocelin was

not summoned, but he went with the others, he says) " raising up the *loculus* with the body, carried it to the altar, and I
lent thereto my sinful hand to help.   Now we all began to
think that the abbot would exhibit the coffin to the people,
and bring forth the sacred body before all of us ; but we
were sadly deceived, for the abbot named twelve monks to
carry out the completion of the sacred task."   Several of
the twelve were versed in carpentry.

The convent being all asleep, the twelve named, clothed
in their albs, with the abbot, assembled at the altar and took
the *loculus* from the shrine and laid it on a table in the

church and made ready for unfastening the lid. The abbot said it was among his prayers to look once upon the body of his patron. When with difficulty the lid was removed, all the twelve save two—the sacristan Hugo, and Walter the medicus—were ordered to draw back. Only the abbot and the two were privileged to look in. This is what they saw.

" The coffin was so filled with the king's body, that even a needle could hardly be put between the head and the wood, or between the feet and the wood. The head lay united to the body,* somewhat raised by a small pillow; the abbot bending down found a silken wrapper veiling the whole body, and then a linen cloth of wondrous whiteness, and over the head was spread another very fine piece of silk, and beneath all these they found the holy body all swathed in linen—but here the abbot paused and said he durst not proceed further or look upon the sacred flesh naked.

" Taking the head between his hands, he then spake softly—' Glorious martyr St. Edmund, blessed be the hour wherein thou wast born. Glorious martyr, turn it not to my destruction, though I, miserable sinner, do touch thee, for thou knowest my devotion.' Then he touched the eyes and the nose which was very massive and prominent, and then he touched the breast and the arms, and placed his fingers between the fingers of the saint, and he touched the toes and counted them. Then the abbot called the other monks who had been assisting, and a very few others who had stolen in the dead of night into the church, and these looked in, and so did John of Dice, a monk who with the vestry keepers had climbed up into the roof. All these clearly saw these things.

" When all was reverently finished the *loculus* was closed

---

* This is rather indefinite, for presently we are told of the abbot " taking the head between his hands."

again and placed in the gorgeously embellished shrine; and when the monks came into the church to chaunt matins and perceived what had been done, all who had not seen these things were very sorrowful, saying among themselves, ' We have been sadly deceived.'

" After matins the abbot called them all to the altar, and showing them what had been done, told them how it was not permissible or fit to invite the whole number of the brethren to the sight of such things. At hearing of which we all wept, and in tears sang ' Te Deum laudamus,' and then we rung the choir-bell." *

From that night in the dim torch-light when Abbot Samson and some of his monks looked on the body of Edmund, king and martyr, around which so great and varied a life had gathered, no human eye, we believe, has ever been permitted to gaze on the loved and venerated remains. All through the Middle Ages royal pilgrimages were ever and anon made to the famous shrine. Among these the visits of King Henry III., Edward I. and his Queen, Edward II., Edward III., Richard II. and Henry VI. (the last making a lengthened stay in the abbey precincts), were the most noticeable.

Devotion to St. Edmund and the love of prayer at his shrine continued among the people without any sign of diminution for several hundred years. It was a popular and loved resort for pilgrims until the Reformation swept away shrine and abbey.

A strange and apparently baseless tradition relates how Prince Louis of France, A.D. 1216, during the civil wars in

---

* "What a scene," writes Carlyle, " shining luminous, effulgent, as the lamps of St. Edmund do, through the dark night, the convent all asleep; yes! there, sure enough, is the martyred body of Edmund, who, nobly doing what he liked with his own, was slain three hundred years ago, and a noble awe surrounds the memory of him, symbol and promoter of many other right noble things."

the days of Henry III., plundered the abbey of St. Edmund, and secretly carried away the *loculus* with the sacred body, leaving the empty shrine intact. But on any such theft the abbey records are absolutely silent. In A.D. 1631, more than four hundred years after Jocelin's death, we hear that the body of St. Edmund was in the crypt of St. Servin at Toulouse, in a stone coffin, unnoticed and unhonoured.

During the year 1628 and for three years following, the city of Toulouse had been ravaged by a terrible visitation of the plague; all the efforts made by the provincial authorities to stamp out the dreadful disease were attended with failure.

It was at last suggested that the body of a great saint lay in the cathedral of St. Servin forgotten and neglected. The leading citizens of Toulouse met, and made a solemn vow publicly to honour the English martyr-king, whose body tradition asserted had been removed from its original resting-place in England to a vault beneath the cathedral.

The solemn vow was publicly made, and the Toulouse story relates that after the vow the plague was stayed. The carrying out of the vow was delayed for some thirteen years, but in A.D. 1644 search was made by the Archbishop of Toulouse and the Chapter of St. Servin, and in the crypt of the cathedral, in a small vault on the west side, a large altar stone was discovered, in front of which was the inscription—

'icy repose le venerable Corps de Sainct Edmond Martyr Roy d'Angleterre

The coffin was opened, and a heap of bones with a skull lying upon them were found within. These were carefully put together, and were found to constitute almost an entire skeleton.

Did these mouldering remains represent the incorrupt and perfect body, the body so carefully wrapped and probably embalmed, of the saint-king Jocelin tells us about in his picture of the night scene in the abbey when Samson opened the sacred *loculus?*

These sad relics were carefully gathered together, and reverently placed in a costly silver shrine provided by the grateful city. The bones of the martyr-king (were they his?) were, with much ceremony and pomp, exposed for veneration for several days after they had been placed in their silver coffer, and we read how enormous crowds visited the cathedral to gaze upon the shrine which contained the supposed remains of the saint, to whose powerful intercession they believed they owed their deliverance from the plague.

The shrine was subsequently replaced in the crypt of St. Servin with extraordinary ceremony in the presence of the Archbishop, the Chapter of the cathedral, and the members of the Parliament of Toulouse.

At the Dissolution, in A.D. 1539, when the abbey was condemned and all its treasures confiscated, the commissioners of Henry VIII. reported that among the beautiful and costly things which they found in the abbey church was "a rich shrine, very cumberous to deface."

The body had apparently disappeared, for no mention is made of it, or of the ancient *loculus* for so many centuries its home. Is it possible that the strange French story of the theft of the body by Prince Louis in the thirteenth century is really true, and that the mouldering relics discovered in the seventeenth century in the vault of St. Servin were, after all, the bones of the English saint? Or was the *loculus* heedlessly and irreverently tossed aside by these rough officers as a thing possessing no intrinsic value, and the sacred ashes scattered to the four winds? Or, when the storm-cloud of destruction was about to burst over the noble abbey, was the coffin with its hallowed contents, before the surrender of the

monastery, reverently taken from beneath its gold and jewelled canopy, and by the loving hands of sorrowful men buried
deep beneath the abbey floor, there to rest until another and a
brighter day for the ancient house of St. Edmund should dawn?

We know this happened to such hallowed reliques in other
places.* It is surely more than probable that some such
pious care at the last preserved the poor remains of the
sainted East Anglian king, for so many centuries the object
of awe and veneration, from wanton, heedless sacrilege.

And some of us, as we wander through the sad and de-
serted ruins of what was once the fairest of our English abbeys,
love to think that beneath the deep matted grass, so thickly
strewn with shapeless piles of broken stones, not far from the
holy spot where the now desecrated altar of the great church
once stood, rests—possibly in a rough-hewn vault—the coffin
which is still guarding the sacred treasure of the body of the
martyr-king, loved by many generations of Englishmen.

　　*　　　*　　　*　　　*　　　*

We know very little of the motives which influenced men
in their attachment through centuries to the strange " cultus "
of St. Edmund, though in such a study as this, any details
which may serve to increase our scanty knowledge here must
possess a peculiar interest.

St. Edmund was evidently feared as well as loved. The
wrath of the king was evidently dreaded, though his power-

---

* Notably at Durham, where we know that St. Cuthbert's body was in the
supreme hour of danger removed from its shrine and solemnly re-interred, and
the secret of the new grave carefully handed down from the Reformation period to
our own day. It is to this that Sir Walter Scott refers in his striking lines in
" Marmion," canto ii., 14—

> " There deep in Durham's Gothic shade
> His reliques are in secret laid,
> 　But none may know the place,
> Save of his holiest servants three,
> Deep sworn to solemn secrecy,
> 　Who share that wondrous grace."

The names of the three who are the holders of the Durham secret in 1892 were
recently told me.

ful advocacy was courted at the throne of the King of kings. The curious student is struck with the aspect of his more famous miracles.

King Sweyn, who would have injured Edmund's abbey, and who openly defied his power, he slew. Abbot Leofstan, who with great reverence dared to touch his body, was punished with paralysis in the offending hands. Herfast, bishop of Elmham, while speaking of the injuries he was proposing to inflict on the holy house of Edmund, was struck in the eye with the overhanging branch of a tree, and for a long period suffered from a partial blindness, and although after a protracted repentance he was healed, the bishop bore for ever the scar of the punishment. Prince Eustace, son of King Stephen, who insultingly ravaged the farms of the monastery, was seized with a strange madness and died.

One of Carlyle's most brilliant chapters begins thus: " Of St. Edmund's fearful avengements have they not an instance before their eyes? He that will go to Reading monastery may find there, now tonsured into a penitent monk, the once proud Henry of Essex (standard-bearer of England in the time of Henry II.), and discern how St. Edmund punishes, terribly, yet with mercy."

Abbot Samson, his devoted and earnest servant, at the famous translation of the body in the solemn night-scene related above, thus deprecates his saint's wrath: " Glorious martyr, turn it not to my perdition that I have dared to touch thee, thou servant of God."

Whatever value we may attach to the Toulouse traditions, this much is certain. The archbishop and the dignitaries of St. Servin, faithful to the old memory of the fearfulness of Edmund, in some way connected the long-continued plague which desolated their fair city with the English saint's wrath at the neglect with which his earthly remains were treated.

M

## CHAPTER I.

THE road between Gloucester and the old storied town of Tewkesbury is unmistakably English in its character. The landscape, always pretty, occasionally beautiful, is made up of forest and river, distant hills and wooded plains. The colouring, on a summer or autumn day, is just what so often meets the eye, especially in the southern midlands — the varied greens of orchard and woods passing imperceptibly into the grey-blue of the distant hills, all half-veiled, half-revealed by the tender sun-lit mists which are the peculiar charm of the atmosphere in the lands of the Severn sea. It is a very fair but not an exciting scene; but stirring memories of old days are not wanting on this quiet English road. Behind there is Gloucester, with its noble cathedral and massive, graceful tower—the scene of so many great events in bygone years— the favourite home of the Norman and Plantagenet kings.

There are the hills close by where folk-lore tells us Saxon Alfred fought for the homes and hearths of his people. There is Deerhurst, where kings older than even Alfred worshipped. The silver Severn, winding in and out of the woods, still washes Olney Island, where Cnut and Edmund Ironside met and divided England between Dane and Saxon. There are the green fields and hedges where the long and weary War of the Roses was at last decided in what is still called the " Bloody Meadow."

So the stranger quietly wanders on through these still and now peaceful scenes, past the " Bloody Meadow " outside old Tewkesbury town, past little houses and bright gardens, past old thatched cottages, till, close by him on his right in the midst of green fields, seemingly alone in its solitary grandeur, rises up a mighty silver-grey abbey, so vast in its proportions that the eye at first can scarcely grasp its exquisite details, or take in its strange unearthly colouring. It needs no explanation. It tells its own story.

The stranger who looks on it for the first time feels he is in the presence of something which is older far than Tudor or Stuart, older even than the red or white rose of Lancaster or of York. He feels that that grey-coloured massive abbey was probably the work of some of those mighty builders who called themselves friends and counsellors of the Conqueror and his brilliant, evil son Rufus; that under the shadow of those walls, coloured as only the Severn storms of eight hundred years can colour, many an eventful scene must have passed in the early days of the Plantagenet princes; that within prayers must have been said and hymns sung by the sons and daughters of men who had to expiate the cruel slaughter of Hastings and the untold miseries brought on hapless Saxon England. Perhaps none of our English abbeys, and only a few even of our great cathedrals, contain the materials of a story like that which Tewkesbury possesses.

*Old House, Tewkesbury.*

Roughly speaking, for four hundred years, that is from the epoch of the Norman Conquest till the close of mediæval times at the Reformation, it was the abbey-home of one of the proudest and most powerful of the Norman baronial families. The first of these great lords built it and endowed it. His children and his children's children loved to enrich it and adorn it; in life they dwelt under its shadow, in death they well-nigh all were laid to sleep beneath its traceried roof, gleaming with dusky gold. They sleep there still all around the great altar; two rows of little stone or marble slabs mark some of the hallowed graves of a long line of Despensers, De Clares, and Beauchamps. Round the fair sanctuary, ruined though it be and defaced, but still lovely in its scarred beauty, graceful chauntries keep their perpetual watch and ward over the remains of the more famous of the lords of Tewkesbury. The chronicles of the abbey, the half-defaced inscriptions on the tombs, tell us the story of the nobles who sleep in this historic church; it is a comment on the way men lived then in "Merrie England." "For some four centuries most of the heirs of the lordly houses of Fitz-Hamon and De Clare, Despenser and Beauchamp, were laid

to rest—some few after peaceful deaths, four of them bruised
and battered in the battlefield, four sent thither by the axe or
the halter, some in early youth, but none reaching old age—
within the walls of the choir of Tewkesbury."

One of the most famous and widely-read stories of the
latter half of the present century has for its scene the quiet
town which boasts as its chief glory—it may be said its only

*The Bell Hotel, " Abel Fletcher's " House, Tewkesbury.*

glory—the stately abbey which is the subject of this little
study. The simple plot of the story is laid in the quiet old-
world streets, by the banks of the twin streams that wind
through the grassy meadows which encircle the now sleepy
town. The scene of the home-like drama is never removed
more than a few miles distant. The reader is familiarised with
every aspect of the pleasant English landscape—the distant
blue hills, the neighouring red and purple orchards, the bright

green water-meadows, the old dusky timber-framed houses of the time-worn historic town-village. But while all these fair but everyday surroundings are used again and again to make up the bright still picture of a pure and well-nigh perfect English home, strange to say the writer of "John Halifax" scarcely notices the principal feature of the scenery of her romance. Once or twice in the course of the narrative the abbey is mentioned, its sweet chimes possibly receiving a passing word, its grey lichen-covered walls perhaps here and there alluded to. But the abbey — that grey mighty pile, with its wealth of storied tombs, with its stirring incidents, with its deathless tradition, stretching over four hundred eventful years, from the Battle of Hastings to the battle of Tewkesbury—awoke no responsive echo in the heart of "John Halifax."

When "John Halifax" was written there was less interest by far felt than in the present day in those ancient reliques of an almost forgotten past. Abbey and cathedral and old parish church were left year after year much as our fathers had left them — winter storms and the slow decay of time worked their will; but the change was very gradual: *without*, grey-green moss and coloured lichen supplied the place here of a fallen pinnacle, there of a broken image; *within*, a curious confusion of Tudor destruction and partial Stuart restoration, in numberless instances made up a quaint, almost a picturesque interior.

Then came the age of enthusiastic restoration. Much that was beautiful and inimitable was ruthlessly swept away through ignorance and misplaced zeal; much though was certainly well and skilfully repaired and preserved. It is not always easy now, without careful study, to distinguish between what is old and what is new. Now well-nigh every village has its neat and pretty church—many of them homes of prayer built in the days of the Plantagenet kings—each church with its Early English or Perpendicular windows, apparently dating from the last ten or fifteen years, filled with modern stained glass; each with its white pillared aisles; its wooden benches, more or less skilfully carved; its little chancel, with new and glistening tiles; its reverently-adorned holy table—all telling the story of many earnest and devout worshippers, though not always of wise or learned archæologists.

Our proud cathedrals and abbey churches, in the great revival of all Church thought and work, were especially cared for; and, with rare exceptions, in these great monuments of expiation and piety the work of renovation and preservation has been admirably carried out, nowhere more conspicuously so than in the noble abbey the subject of the present study.

Never since the day of dissolution and destruction—more than three and a half centuries ago—has the great house of God in Tewkesbury shown so much of its old glorious beauty as it does to-day. Of course it is all sadly changed. The colour and the gold which in old Plantagenet days lit up with a strange rich beauty the stern white vista of Norman arch and rounded column have all disappeared; much of the splendid and gorgeous colouring which once clothed the graceful Decorated and Perpendicular tracery of the eastern limb of the great church has faded away; the jewelled shrines are bare—some, alas! are in ruins; the roofs, once bright with gold, and flaming with scarlet and purple, are now but scantily adorned. But yet, even in its partly ruined and defaced state it is reverently cared for, and its serene scarred beauty is still a delight to gaze on.

Its foundation dates far, far back. Tradition refers it to the first half of the eighth century. It was founded no doubt in the same age which witnessed the building of the neighbouring abbeys of Gloucester and Pershore, when Christianity

was beginning slowly but surely to win its way after the first
desolating storm of the fury of the Saxon invader had somewhat spent itself.   This wild storm of heathen invaders in
the Mercian country was more devastating in its effects than
perhaps is generally supposed.   For instance, the once
wealthy and flourishing Roman-British cities of Glevum
(Gloucester) and Aquæ Solis (Bath), after the invasion of
Ceawlin the Saxon, apparently remained in ruins and un-
inhabited for a century.

The story speaks of the first religious house being built
in the immediate neighbourhood of a primitive little chapel
erected by a holy hermit named Theoc.   Nothing is known
of Theoc's life and work.   The well-known name, however, is
commonly derived from this old missionary, " Theocsbury "
subsequently passing into the modern Tewkesbury.   " Theo-
kusburia " is the common way of writing the name in the
Middle Ages.   Others have derived the word from two
imaginary Dukes or Duces, Oddo and Doddo, who lived in
the eighth century, " Duces-bury."   Another derivation
which has been suggested is yet more fanciful, viz., from the
Greek word " Theotokos," because the church was originally
dedicated to the Blessed Virgin Mary.

Beyond its bare existence little is recorded of the story of the
original priory. Nothing now remains of the old Saxon religious
house, or of the priory church.   Before the Norman Conquest
the Anglo-Saxon monastery and church of Tewkesbury were
of small importance, and in Edward the Confessor's days were
subject to the Dorsetshire Abbey of Cranbourn ; and of the
early Saxon buildings there is not the slightest trace remaining.   The last Anglo-Saxon lord of Tewkesbury was that
great theign Brihtric, who in the days of King Edward
possessed enormous estates in the neighbourhood of the
Severn.   This Brihtric was a distant connection of the king,
and in early life—so runs the story—incurred the bitter

enmity of Matilda, then Princess of Flanders, by refusing her hand in marriage. When Matilda became queen of conquered England, she asked and obtained, as part of her share of the conquest, the lands of the Saxon Brihtric. Thus Tewkesbury after her death reverted to the Crown.

# CHAPTER II.

SOME think that in Tewkesbury Abbey we have the most solemn and impressive interior of all the English churches. It belongs to the early years of the great church-building age in England, which dates from some twenty years after the Battle of Hastings, and which reached far into the reign of the Angevin King Henry II.—a period, roughly speaking, of nearly one hundred years, in which short interval more stately cathedrals, abbeys, and religious houses were built than in the three to four centuries of Saxon rule that preceded it, or in the eight centuries of Plantagenet and Tudor, Stuart and Guelph domination which followed.

This remarkable wave of church-building, which seems in so marked a fashion to have especially affected England A.D. 1080—1160, is undoubtedly to be traced in many instances to a feeling of remorse on the part of many of the Norman conquerors for the terrible sufferings they had inflicted on the noble Anglo-Saxon nation. Ordericus Vitalis tells us how the dying Conqueror was heard to say, " Of how many thousands of young as well as of old belonging to that illustrious England, have I been the unhappy slayer!" The same sad thought was in the minds of not a few of his too faithful followers. To some such desire to atone for terrible wrong done was owing the foundation of the lordly Abbey of Tewkesbury.

The "honour of Gloucester," which included a large portion of the beautiful vale of the Severn, was bestowed by Rufus upon a great Norman noble, his kinsman, Robert Fitz-Hamon, Seigneur of Cardiff and of many another Norman and Saxon home, who had distinguished himself by splendid gallantry in the long border wars between the Normans and the Welshmen. It has been suggested that it was this Fitz-Hamon who had the charge of the ill-fated Duke Robert of Normandy, the Conqueror's eldest son, and that his must have been the hideous task of superintending the placing of the red-hot iron bowl before Robert's eyes, and the carrying out of Henry Beauclerc's terrible sentence of blinding, early in the twenty years' captivity passed by Robert in Cardiff Castle.* The brilliant Crusader Duke Robert—after his sad life of storm alternated with brief gleams of sunshine, closing with those long weary years of hopeless darkness—sleeps his long sleep as he wished, in the great Abbey of Gloucester, in front of the high altar.

Fitz-Hamon,† in addition to his many honours, received the hand of the Conqueror's niece Sybilla : his descendants, who ruled in Tewkesbury nearly four hundred years, were thus doubly connected with the royal house of the Conquerors of England. Long before the abbey which he planned with so much care, as his offering of expiation, was complete, the Norman noble passed into the silent land, where victors and vanquished would meet before the same awful tribunal.

---

* This is, however, doubtful, for Duke Robert was only taken captive A.D. 1106, in which year tradition seems to assert Robert Fitz-Hamon received his death wound, either at Tinchebrai or at the siege of Falaise.

† The style adopted by Fitz-Hamon was, Robert Fitz-Hamon by the grace of God Prince of Glamorgan, Earl of Corbeil, Baron of Thonguy and Granville, Lord of Gloucester, Bristol, Tewkesbury, and Cardiff, &c.

His remains lie on the north side of the choir, not far from the high altar.  A stone which once contained a brass marks the exact spot where the leaden shroud was found.  The tomb is enclosed in a rich Perpendicular chauntry, erected at the end of the fourteenth century.  The founder of the abbey was conspicuous in those days of gloomy suspicion and perpetual wars for his unwavering loyalty to the Conqueror, to Rufus and Henry I.  The great lord of the marches of Glamorgan was a trusted and intimate friend of each of the first three Norman sovereigns.  He was with Rufus at his hunting lodge in the New Forest on that sad August day which closed the Red King's life.  Early in the morning he roused the sleeping king with tidings of a warning brought to him as the dream of a holy monk beyond the sea, and besought his dread master not to hunt that day.  Rufus—so runs the true story—laughed, but bade Fitz-Hamon send a truly royal guerdon to the dreaming monk, and so far followed his friend's advice that he put off his sport till the eventide.

Before the evening came another urgent prayer to the king from Serlo, the well-known Gloucester abbot, the friend of the Conqueror and of Lanfranc, not to adventure his royal person in the New Forest's leafy glades just then ; but Rufus was bent on indulging his wayward fancy, and followed by Fitz-Hamon and some half-dozen Norman nobles, he mounted his horse, and that same day in the cool evening hour, galloped away from his friends " into the depths of the forests, through the chequered gleams of transparent green, through the pleasant shade, the huge stems of the forest trees shining in the golden light of the setting sun." The lord of Tewkesbury and a few others hastened after their royal master, whom they lost sight of in the forest glades. " No man ever owned that he had spoken again to the dread Norman king.  No man owned to having again heard the

West Front of Canterbury Abbey

voice of Rufus, except in the inarticulate agonies of death.
Fitz-Hamon and Gilbert de Aquila found him expiring,
stretched on the ground, within the walls of the ruined
church, just below the Malwood Castle, transpierced by the
shaft of a Norman arbalist, the blood gurgling in his throat.
Fitz-Hamon and Gilbert de Aquila tried to pray with him,
but in vain.''*

The founder of our abbey continued his faithful service to
King Henry Beauclerc until, six or seven years later, the fatal
arrow from the defenders of Falaise put a term at once to life
and service.

Great and powerful as was Fitz-Hamon, his successor,
who married the daughter of the founder of the abbey, and
finished his work, filled a yet more prominent place in the
history of his day. The founder left no son to inherit his
proud name and vast inheritance. King Henry Beauclerc
claimed his daughter and heiress Maboly (Mabel) for his
favourite son Robert. Robert's mother was the beautiful
Nesta,† a daughter of Rhys ap Tudor, the last native prince
of Glamorgan, who, strangely enough, had been slain by
Mabel's father Fitz-Hamon. This Robert was perhaps the
noblest of all the early Norman barons. During a long and
eventful life, he was conspicuous not only for his great powers
as a general and statesman, but for his spotless, chivalrous
character.

The Chronicler (Robert of Gloucester) gives us an interesting specimen of "les mœurs contemporaines" in his
account of " How a High-born Norman Heiress received the
King's overtures in behalf of his Son." The young lady was

---

* Palgrave, " Normandy and England," vol. iv., ch. xii.

† The later " Brut " (Layamon—end of century xii.) asserts this, and Palgrave,
with most historians, accepts the usual tradition. Professor Freeman, however,
who allows that Beauclerc was the father of Earl Robert, doubts if Princess Nesta
was his mother.

not carried away by any mere romantic notions of love for the nameless young knight, *sans peur et sans reproche* as he seems to have been, but evidently was determined, before she accepted him as her husband, to secure his future position.

In the Chronicle,* Lady Mabel addresses King Henry Beauclerc thus—

> "Sir, shee saide, i'll wote your herte upon me is
> More for myne heritage than for myselfe, I wis ;
> And such heritage as ich have, it weer to me greet shame
> To take a Lorde but he had any surname : "

The king replies to her—

> " Damoiseill, quoth the Kyng, thou seest well in this case,
> Sir Robert Fitz-Hame thi fader's name was :
> As fayre a name hee shall have as you may see,
> Sir Robert le Fitz-Roy shall his name be.''

The Lady Mabel asks naturally, " What name shall our children bear? " and the king made answer—

> " Damoiseill, he say'd, thi Lord shall have a name,
> For him and for his heires, fair and without blame ;
> For Robert Erle of Gloucester his name shall be and is ;
> Hee shall be Erle of Gloucester, and his heires, I wis.''

Then Mabel agrees to the marriage.

> ʾ     " Inne this forme, quoth shee, ich wole that all my thying be his."

This was the great Earl Robert of Gloucester—the faithful and chivalrous supporter of his half-sister, the Empress Matilda, Beauclerc's heiress. During the long and bloody wars which followed on the death of King Henry, he was the faithful and true guardian of Matilda and her boy, afterwards the wise and mighty King Henry II.

Notwithstanding his restless, war-filled life, Earl Robert,

* Robert of Gloucester (beginning of fourteenth century), quoted by Mr. Blunt, "Tewkesbury Abbey ; " also by Professor Freeman, " Norman Conquest," vol. v. note BB., appendix.

with the aid of his countess, Fitz-Hamon's heiress, found time
well-nigh to complete the abbey. In A.D. 1123 there was a
stately consecration ceremony; five bishops and a goodly
company of great ecclesiastics and men of note took part in
the solemn function.

The tower, and probably the beautiful west front, were
finished by their son, William Fitzcount. This heir of all
the broad lands of the honour of Gloucester lived in the
more peaceful times when England was under the strong
wise rule of Henry II. He enjoyed his great position and
power for some thirty-six years. But his life was clouded by
the early death of his only son Robert at his castle of
Cardiff. In memory of the dead boy, he and his wife, Avice
de Bellamont of Leicester, built and endowed the great church
and religious house of Keynsham on the Avon, between
Bath and Bristol. Different to the fate of the abbey at
Tewkesbury, which is comparatively little changed since
William Fitzcount and Avice de Bellamont prayed in it
and lived beneath its shadow, Keynsham Abbey is utterly
destroyed.

No son survived to succeed to the lordship of Gloucester
and Tewkesbury. Isabella, the third daughter of William
Fitzcount and Avice de Bellamont, had the ill fortune to
attract Prince John, afterwards the king. The broad lands
of Tewkesbury, in default of a male heir, were in the keeping
of the Crown, and on his marriage with Isabella of Tewkesbury came into possession of Prince John, then Earl of
Moreton. The marriage was an unhappy one, and when John
after some ten years became king, he divorced Isabella;
but on payment of an enormous fine he gave Tewkesbury
and the lordship of Gloucester to her second husband,
Geoffrey Mandeville, Earl of Essex. She died childless, as
did her elder sister Mabel, the wife of Almeric de Montford,
Count d'Evreux. There was yet another sister, Amice, who

*The Bear Inn and Long Bridge, Tewkesbury.*

married Gilbert De Clare, Earl of Hertford, who in right of
his wife, Fitz-Hamon's great granddaughter, became Earl
of Gloucester and Lord of Tewkesbury, A.D. 1221, Henry III.
being king of England.

Thus the golden shield of the De Clares, with its three
red chevrons, came into the abbey of Fitz-Hamon, and for
eighty-nine years the De Clares reigned over the splendid
heritage of the Conqueror's kinsman.

Several of these De Clares lie in a solemn row in front of
the high altar of the abbey between the end of the monks'
stalls and the graves of the Despensers, who occupy a yet
more honourable place of sepulture than the lordly De
Clares, their immediate ancestors. They were a splendid
and a gallant race, these De Clares of Tewkesbury, typical
Norman barons of the highest rank; well is the golden shield

with the three red chevrons known to the student and the antiquary of the Severn lands. In beautiful Worcester, in lordly Gloucester, in storied Tewkesbury, in many an ancient house of God in this old Mercian country, on jewelled windows still faintly glowing with pale gold and dusky red—hues which no modern craftsman can hope to imitate—painted on ruddy tiles worn smooth by the feet of men who lived while the Plantagenets ruled in England, on stone or marble graved with cunning skill by long-forgotten hands, the arms borne by the once-famed house appear again and again. They played too, did this Norman royal-descended house, a distinguished part in the stirring history of these times. The first De Clare, who married the daughter of William, Earl of Pembroke, Marshal of England, whose splendid effigy lies in the round church of the Temple, wrote his name, as did his father also, among those names which will never die in the memory of Englishmen, in the Great Charter the barons wrung at Runnymede from John Plantagenet, the shifty, faithless king. Another, the husband of Princess Joan of Acre, the daughter of Edward I., fought at Evesham. Their son Gilbert fell bravely fighting on the stricken field of Bannockburn. It is this young warrior De Clare of whom Walter Scott sings in the *Lord of the Isles.*

> "' Then prove we if they die or win !
> Bid Gloster's earl the fight begin '—
> Earl Gilbert waved his truncheon high,
> Just as the Northern ranks arose,
> Signal for England's archery,
>   To halt and bend their bows.
>   *     *     *     *     *
> There Gloster plied the bloody sword,
> And Berkeley, Grey, and Hereford."

On the mouldering remains of some of these De Clares men have looked in this generation. When the abbey was restored a few years ago, the stone coffin of Gilbert, who signed Magna Charta, was found. The sides of the stone *loculus* were partly gone, but the dust which once was the stern Norman baron was still there. The heart of his countess, the daughter of the Marshal of England, enclosed in a silver vase, perhaps still lies buried before the high altar. The gorgeous monument, richly decorated with gold, silver, and precious stones, which once marked the resting-place of Earl Richard, who was poisoned in A.D. 1262, has disappeared, but his stone coffin, quite perfect, was found, the bones still preserved lying within. The story of Tewkesbury tells us how his bowels were buried at Canterbury and his heart at Tunbridge.

The remains of the last of the male De Clares, Gilbert III., Earl of Gloucester, who fell fighting gallantly at Bannockburn, were seen when in 1875 the choir pavement was restored. In a shallow grave of very fine masonry, the skeleton, almost perfect, remained. The bones lay undisturbed, but uncoffined, upon two slabs of hard blue stone.

The lordship of Tewkesbury and the patronage of the famous abbey, on the death of Earl Gilbert III., became the inheritance of his sister Eleanor, who married the ill-fated Hugh le Despenser the younger, who on his marriage was created Earl of Gloucester. For nearly a century (ninety-three years) the illustrious house of Despenser reigned in Tewkesbury, A.D. 1321 to A.D. 1414.

This Hugh le Despenser the younger was one of the few who remained faithful to the fallen fortunes of the unhappy King Edward II. He fell into the hands of Isabella the queen and her favourite Mortimer, and as a guerdon for his loyalty to her hated husband was hanged on a lofty gallows in Hereford and then quartered. The mutilated remains of Hugh le Despenser were distributed to various towns, no doubt to be displayed on the gates. Froissart tells us that the head was sent to London.

There is a ghastly picture of this execution in one of the Froissart MSS., in which Lord Despenser is depicted as fastened to a high ladder, a richly dressed group of Isabella's courtiers is gazing at him, while the tormentor is

*High Street, Tewkesbury.*

engaged in cutting out his heart, to receive which a fire is burning at the foot of the ladder. In the reaction which ensued shortly after, on the accession of Edward III., these sad reliques of the Lord of Tewkesbury were gathered together and brought back to his abbey, and buried, Leland tells us, near the lavatory of the high altar, and a tomb of extraordinary richness was built over the *loculus* which contained them. It is still there, this sad Despenser tomb, behind the sedilia of the altar, beautiful even in its present utter ruin and decay.

These Despensers, during their hundred years of reign at Tewkesbury, were also prominent among the nobles of England. They were proud of the great abbey which threw its broad shadow over their home and vast estate ; and under their care most of the splendid ornaments of the noble pile were planned and executed. It was a great age for ornamental architecture. Amongst these were the groined roof of the nave, the clerestory and roof of the choir, once glittering with gold and elaborate colouring, and the matchless crown of chapels around the glorious choir. Several of the stately tombs of Tewkesbury are marvels of elegance and beauty —tombs which, after centuries of neglect, are still amongst the most interesting and striking in England. The stained glass, which still casts its many-coloured hues on the pavement that covers the ashes of these once famous men, was put up in memory of one or another of these now forgotton lords. Of course these stained windows are much defaced and broken, but strangely enough have suffered less than many of the seemingly imperishable monuments of alabaster and marble erected by the same noble house, and these gem-like windows, with their extraordinary richness and brilliancy of colouring, constitute one of the most conspicuous glories of our abbey.

This illustrious house came to an end in 1415, after nearly a century of possession, and Tewkesbury, lands and abbey, in default of male heirs, passed to Isabella, sister of the last Lord Despenser. She was the great-granddaughter of Edward III., her grandmother being the Princess Joan of Acre. This Isabella Despenser married twice. Her first husband was Richard Beauchamp (de Bello Campo, as the proud name is sometimes written on brasses and tombs), Earl of Abergavenny. From their daughter, Elizabeth Beauchamp, descended the present well-known noble house of Abergavenny. This Richard Beauchamp fought at Agincourt, and for his conspicuous gallantry in the field was created Earl of Worcester. He was killed at the siege of Meaux. They brought him home and buried him in his abbey. This heiress of the Despensers married a second time a yet greater man, a cousin of her first husband, another Richard Beauchamp, Earl of Warwick. He too fought at Agincourt, and subsequently became guardian of the boy-king, Henry VI., and in the end regent of France. He died in Rouen Castle comparatively young. This famous earl sleeps beneath the magnificent and well-known tomb at Warwick. His wife died the same year, and was laid to sleep in the stately abbey near her De Clare and Despenser ancestors. The story speaks of a gorgeous tomb erected over her who had sat under the canopy of the regent of France, but it has disappeared. Her daughter, the Lady Anne, married Warwick, "the Kingmaker," "the last of the Barons," and their child Isabella became the wife of the Duke of Clarence, brother of King Edward IV., and with this Isabella, the last lady of Tewkesbury, the connection of the long and illustrious line of Fitz-Hamon with the abbey was closed.

Her sister Anne, the wife of Prince Edward of Wales, murdered after the battle of Tewkesbury, married the Duke of Gloucester, afterwards Richard III., her first husband's bitterest foe. She died, it is said, by poison.

But the abbey—the home of the vanished race—is with us still, in its old grandeur and majesty; and as the stranger for the first time gazes on those vast simple columns, he feels he is in the presence of a building raised by men who worked under some mighty inspiration — probably the inspiration which taught men, in the first fervour of sorrow for a great national sin, to build as men had never built before, have never built since.

For it is indisputable that most of our grandest cathedrals owe their impressiveness to the Norman element, either from their retaining great portions of the original massive structure, like Gloucester and Durham, or from preserving much of their Norman outline in a later style. Tewkesbury Abbey in its exterior and interior, after well-nigh eight centuries of change and decay, still presents, in spite of the important alterations of the fourteenth century, "with but little change the primitive Norman arrangement, and a general outline representing pretty fairly that of the original building," as designed by the architect of Fitz-Hamon in the days of William Rufus.

The beauty of our abbey is in its way simply matchless as it rises out of the green water-meadows which fringe the Avon and Severn, a mighty pile tenderly coloured with those soft grey hues which only long centuries of wear and tear can paint upon the stones, with its great square tower, so massive, and yet so richly adorned with its rows of intersecting arches and round-headed windows, and the striking chevron ornament cunningly weaved round each little Norman pillar, with its choir much altered from the old plan of Fitz-Hamon, but still in its new form (*new;* it was changed in the days of the Third Edward!) perfectly lovely with its coronet of chapels, and curious delicate parapet crowning the east end like a fringe of petrified lace.

Within, travelling along the avenue of mighty pillars, the glory which the two Severn minsters, Gloucester and Tewksbury, alone possess, the eye rests upon the sumptuous beauty of the choir, utterly unlike the choir of Gloucester, but possessing a loveliness of its own ; seen from the western door, there meets the eye a very confusion of fretted roof and carved shrine, all dimly lit by the famous windows, the offering of the widow of the murdered Hugh Despenser the younger, with their wealth of brilliant colouring.

But our abbey is something more than a noble and exquisite church which charms and delights the eye, more than a venerable pile which affords an ever fresh and varying interest to the archæologist and the architect. It was, we remember, for some four hundred eventful, stirring years, the prayer-house, the sanctuary, the oratory, the tomb of a long line of those mighty Norman barons who, from the day of the battle of Hastings till the day of the battle of Tewkesbury, were at once the strength and the terror of the English people and their king. The first Norman lord of Tewkesbury was Fitz-Hamon, the Conqueror's kinsman. The last lord of the great abbey was the Earl of Warwick, "the King-maker," whom history knows as "the last of the Barons."

# CHAPTER III.

THE pale grey-white nave—with its vast round columns —cold and severe, yet inexpressibly imposing and solemn— is scarcely changed since that dedication morning more than seven and a half centuries ago. There were gleams of gold and colour then on the timber roofs, in the little chapels, the aisles, and on the many altars ; but, generally speaking, it is the same stately vista which meets the eye now as that on which Robert and Mabel, and many a knight and noble of Henry Beauclerc's court, gazed in the days of the Norman kings of England.

Yes, it is the same vista of great round pillars which King Beauclerc, the Conqueror's son, looked on. It is the same solemn house in which King Henry and discarded Nesta's son prayed. It was the loved oratory for four hundred years of that long and noble line which sprang from Henry's son and royally descended Fitz-Hamon's heiress. It is also the great tomb in which this historic race is sleeping their last unbroken sleep. It was too the abbey church for centuries of a busy, crowded, and industrious Benedictine monastery. What thoughts come thronging on us as we pace in mute reverence the pavement of the holy house of Tewkesbury !

*Shrine and Loculus in which the mutilated remains of Hugh le Despenser the younger were deposited.*

Under our feet moulders the hallowed dust of chivalrous men whose style and title have been with us as household words since our school-boy days. Here is the stone which covers the coffin of one who was the Conqueror's familiar friend and kinsman; close by him lies the stern patriot baron who, with his mailed hand, signed Magna Charta; before us sleeps the gallant knight who fell in the front rank at Bannockburn—Earl Gilbert, "Gloster's earl" of Scott's *Lord of the Isles;* just at our side, beneath a gorgeous canopy, overshadowing a knight with folded hands and up-turned face, sleeps the man who carried the proud English standard for King Edward at Cressy; close by, beneath what was once a splendid tomb, now but a scarred and defaced ruin, are buried the mutilated remains of Hugh le

Despenser the younger, the faithful friend of poor discrowned
Edward II.; all round the rich and graceful choir, before
the high altar, behind in the solemn ambulatory which
fringes presbytery and choir, lie thickly strewn about, abbot
and prior, Earls of Clare and their countesses, Lords
Despenser and their noble consorts, and many a mighty
Neville and Beauchamp.     There too lies the young king
of Wight—the only "crowned" noble in the history of
England, the boy favourite of Henry VI., who gave him the
royal ornaments and title.

One vault, pre-eminent in sad historic interest, is the
last home of Isabel Neville, the murdered daughter of the
once mighty Warwick; by her side rest the bones of one
more faithful to her in death than in life, of royal Clarence,
Edward IV.'s gay and fickle brother—"false, fleeting, perjured Clarence."     Below the lantern of the great central
tower, a little tablet, let into the stone pavement, tells us
how in that spot was buried, after the bloody fight of Tewkesbury, the body of the poor little Red Rose Prince of Wales,
the luckless son of the unhappy saint-king Henry VI.; foully
murdered—says the current legend—after the battle, in the
old house near what was once the Market Cross, scarce a
bow-shot from the abbey.

What sacred pile among our many storied cathedrals,
save perhaps Westminster and Winchester, and the Metro-
politan church at Canterbury, possesses a like wealth of
memories?   One of the saddest and most terrible of these
memories will never be forgotten.   Once the hallowed pavement of the sacred abbey was the scene of a terrible
massacre.   The Battle of Tewkesbury was fought literally
under the shadow of the great church.

The husband of the last of the line of Fitz-Hamon the
Conqueror's kinsman, who was to reign at Tewkesbury,
Warwick the King-maker, had fallen on the field of Barnet,

A.D. 1471. King Edward IV., perhaps the greatest general of his age, determined to crush out, without an hour's delay, the remains of the Lancastrian party; by forced marches from royal Windsor he overtook the Red Rose army as they were retreating into the fastnesses of South Wales, where the house of Lancaster had still many friends. Queen Margaret, the young Prince Edward of Wales, and the surviving Lancastrian lords, on the point of crossing the river, turned to bay beneath the grey old abbey by the Severn waters.

The forces of Queen Margaret were dispirited, wearied with harassing marches, and unskilfully led, nor, as the terrible scene of Lord Wenlock's death suggests, was the spectre of treachery absent from the Red Rose ranks. The Yorkists were flushed with their recent victory at Barnet, and were commanded by a really able general. The battle soon became a rout. In the "Bloody Meadow," only a little distance from the abbey, three thousand men, mostly soldiers of Queen Margaret, lay dead on the field. The defeated Lancastrians retreated on the abbey. The slain, we read, lay thick among the graves in the churchyard, and the terrible carnage was continued even in the sacred building.

For a month after the battle, no prayer was said or hymn sung in the holy house. It had been polluted with blood, and was therefore ceremonially cleansed and formally re-dedicated. The beautiful chauntries of Beauchamp and Despenser were filled with wounded and dying men. The abbot in front of the high altar, with the Host in his hands, in vain besought the wild Yorkist soldiers to stay their slaying hands. The massacre in the abbey was only stayed by the arrival of King Edward. The Duke of Somerset, Lord Devonshire, and other Red Rose leaders were taken prisoners clinging to the altar; Prince Edward of Wales surrendered on the battlefield.

That same woeful May afternoon the young and gallant

*Tewkesbury.— The Cross.—House where Prince Edward is supposed to have been murdered.*

Edward of Wales was led into Edward IV.'s presence: the king after the battle had taken up his lodging in an old timbered house in Church Street. The Yorkist sovereign demanded of his royal prisoner how he durst so presumptuously enter into his realm with banner displayed. The prince answered that he came to recover his father's kingdom. Angered at the bold reply, the king struck him with his gauntlet, on which the Dukes of Gloucester and Clarence, who were standing by with Lords Dorset and Hastings, stabbed the helpless boy-prince with their daggers. *His blood still stains the floor** of the

---

* There is another tradition which says Prince Edward was simply slain while flying from the battle towards the town. This is well discussed by Mr. Bazeley, rector of Matson, in his careful paper on the Battle of Tewkesbury. The learned local antiquaries, Mr. Blunt and Mr. Symonds, rector of Pendock, prefer to keep

room. They buried him in the stately abbey, just under the central tower; a little brass tablet marks the supposed spot. The day but one after (Monday, May 6th, A.D. 1471), the Duke of Somerset and fourteen of the Lancastrian chiefs were brought before a court, of which the Duke of Gloucester was president, and summarily condemned and executed. Tradition says King Edward IV. watched the bloody death-scene from the window of his lodging in Church Street. They were buried, with other notable persons who fell in the battle, in St. James's Chapel of the abbey.

No monument or tablet marks the grave of these unfortunate Lancastrian chiefs. On the 22nd of that same month of May, Henry VI. was "found dead" in his prison-room in the Tower, and the long Wars of the Roses were at an end.

Among the Lancastrian spoils Tewkesbury fell to the share of the Duke of Clarence, brother of Edward IV. He had a claim to the old Despenser and Warwick estates through his wife Isabel, the daughter of the fallen Warwick the King-maker. The next five years, filled with memories of past treachery, with present jealousies, and a future all dark and uncertain, must have been a feverish, unhappy time both for Clarence and Isabella. Two children of the luckless

to the old acccount as above given. Mr. Symonds, however, doubts if the Duke of Clarence and the others actually did the deed. The local tradition has but little varied. Hume and Lingard repeat the same account ; the latter, however, placing the scene in Edward's tent. Shakespeare, in his well-known reference to the event, places the scene of the prince's death in " the *field* outside Tewkesbury ; " but his actors in the tragedy include the same royal group of brothers. The name of the knight who took Edward prisoner, Sir Richard Croft, is preserved. It is scarcely probable that one of such exalted rank would have been heedlessly killed in the *mêlée*, for doubtless he bore some of the insignia which would have marked his rank. At the foot of a pillar north-west of the tower, lately some workmen employed in the restoration of the abbey floor turned up the upper portion of a coffin lid, on which was still remaining the greater part of a tilting helmet. The colour, which yet remained, represented the Prince of Wales's plume as it used to be delineated in mediæval times. The coffin, it is most probable, was the one in which the poor young prince's remains were laid.

union survived.  Both eventually perished on Tower Hill.
The hapless Duchess of Clarence died in 1477 in the
monastery infirmary.

   They buried her in a vault just behind the high altar.  A
fortnight after she had been laid in the Clarence vault,
the body of the weak and wicked duke was placed beside her.
He was accused of treason and other crimes, and put to
death by his brother the king; the well-known story tells us he
" was drowned in a butt of malmsey."   The duke's body was
brought to Tewkesbury Abbey by Edward IV.'s direction.
In a letter from Dr. Langton to the prior of Christ Church,
Canterbury (1478), we read how the king " assigned certain
lords to go with the body of the Dukys of Clarence to
Teuxbury, where he shall be buryid, the kyng intendis to
do right worshipfully for his sowle."

   The Clarence vault has been often examined.  In 1829
there were pieces of a wood coffin lying about covered with
what looked like red velvet.   In 1876, an eye-witness writes:
" The masonry of the vault is fine, the floor paved with tiles
(heraldic).   The stone coffin full of very clear water.   One
small perfect skull and fragments of another lay in the coffin,
and many bones were also lying in the water."

# CHAPTER IV.

## THE END OF THE ABBEY.

THE great church is strangely quiet now; the houses of
De Clare and Despenser belong to the history of England,
while the families of Neville and Beauchamp—whose ancestors still seem to keep watch and ward over the abbey they
loved so well—have no share in the abbey and its broad
lands. The little town of Tewkesbury clusters round the
silver-grey and lichen-covered walls of the old abbey,
scarcely comprehending what a priceless monument of a far-
back past of an almost forgotten England it possesses. The
quaint old village-town has its own peculiar charm, with its
timber-framed ancient houses, but it is something quite apart
from the mighty church, which belongs to another age.
The abbey is, in good truth, reverently cared for, and a little
handful of devout worshippers keep up the holy custom of
perpetual intercession as each morning and evening comes
round; but its original object and purpose was done away with
in the sad zeal of the Reformation, which rooted up wheat
and tares with a strange, unhappy indiscrimination.

This is not the place to attempt an *apologia* either for the
monasteries which were swept away in the course of the second

9

quarter of the sixteenth century, or for the ruthless deeds of
those who suppressed these homes often of earnest prayer
and real learning.   Enough has been written—making due
allowance for the grossest exaggerations—to show that in
some cases the sternest reformer was needed; in all a new
departure in work and activity was imperatively called for,
especially considering the changed condition of student life
mainly owing to the introduction of the printing-press.   For
several centuries great religious houses like Tewkesbury,
belonging to the widespread Benedictine Order, had been
vast manufactories of books.   Probably from these quiet
homes proceeded the vast majority of written volumes in the
centuries which preceded the great invention of Gutenberg.
The Benedictine was often the author, the compiler, the scribe
and the binder.   The very cells where these monks thought
and wrote and worked are still with us in the south walk of the
cloister of our holy house in Gloucester, much as their occu-
pants left them three and a half centuries ago.   These men
were too the great educators of the young.*

Many of the more important of these houses, such as
Gloucester and Tewkesbury, seem to have been perfectly
free from those graver abuses which are so often baselessly
made the subject of the charges levelled at the suppressed
monasteries.

To Tewkesbury the mournful privilege seems to have
been given of being the last of the surrenders to King
Henry VIII.'s commissioners.   All the monastic buildings,
save the Abbot's Lodging, were deemed "superfluous," and
were put down (or scheduled) to be destroyed—including
the glorious abbey.   This was, however, spared.   The fatal

---

* I omit here some of the more "subjective" uses of these great homes of
prayer.   As long as we admit the power of prayer, we can scarcely pass over the
question of the *efficacy* of the "perpetual intercession," not only for their own
souls, but for "all sorts and conditions of men"—an intercession that was every day
and night rising up many times to the Throne from these holy houses.

decision was carried out; this explains the mournful isola-
tion of the mighty pile. The superb cloister, once the rival
of the matchless Gloucester cloister-walks, the vast dormitories, the library, the infirmary and its chapel, the kitchens,
the refectory, the chapter-house, and many another adjunct
of the monastery were ruthlessly pulled down. The
materials when saleable were disposed of; the rest were
carried away and built into farm-houses and buildings, sheds,
and walls. The ruins of a great religious house in many
cases served the neighbouring peasants as a stone quarry for
long years after the suppression.

But the abbey itself, we know, was preserved. The
rescue of this historic church came about in this wise. The
inhabitants of the town of Tewkesbury—in the old days far
more numerous than at present, for then the monastery was
flourishing and a great baron's house was close by—had been
from time immemorial welcomed by the abbey monks in the
great Norman nave, the monks reserving the choir for their
own many services. The abbey nave then was the parish
church of Tewkesbury. The comparatively poor folk of the
town, when the decree of destruction went forth, ransomed
the choir and the monk's end of the great church from the
king, and positively paid a large sum "to the king's highness," according to the royal letters patent authorising the
sale, the parishioners covenanting to bear and find the
reparation of the said church perpetually. This singular
bargain, so much to the honour of the poor Tewkesbury folk,
bears as date the 24th of June and the thirty-fourth year of
King Henry VIII.'s reign.

In Tewkesbury the ten generations who have lived in the
old timber-framed houses of its little streets have kept, at
least in decent repair, the grand old abbey which their
fathers so nobly bought from the rapacious courtiers of
King Henry. This has been no slight burden for so small

a place, for, except St. Alban's Abbey* and the noble minster
church at Beverley, the people of Tewkesbury, numbering
some five thousand, possess in their rescued abbey the
largest parish church in England.    But, until the last few
years, little save bare repairs has been done to the historic
pile.  It was difficult to mar the beauty of Tewkesbury
Abbey.    Still the tasteless work of some of those who
exercised authority over the glorious house did its best to
disfigure the design of Fitz-Hamon and his master-builder,
and to spoil the exquisite fancies of the fourteenth-century
artists.

Hideous galleries were erected, and white-wash was sub-
stituted for the old beautiful colouring and the delicate
gleaming gold; but no real and permanent mischief was
done, and in our day and time—when so many splendid and
successful efforts have been made to restore the old beauty,
and give back colour and light to the ritual and services of
the Church of England, without the old mistakes and errors,
when such pains have been devoted to preserve, and, if
possible, to restore the beautiful fabrics of the pre-Reformation minsters and churches—Tewkesbury Abbey stands in
the forefront of reverent and careful restorations, and in its
cold and severe beauty, sadly marred and defaced though it
be, it gives us some notion of what a noble church was in
the days of our Plantagenet kings.

* St. Alban's has now become the cathedral of an important diocese.

# CHAPTER V.

## THE ARCHITECTURE OF THE ABBEY.

In the last year of the eleventh century Fitz-Hamon and his architect determined to build an entirely new and stately church on the site of the old Saxon foundation. In many respects in its interior arrangement it is almost an exact copy of the Gloucester Abbey, on a slightly smaller scale. Possibly the neighbouring abbey of Pershore resembled it in some details, but of Pershore only a fragment remains; its nave, alas! has disappeared.

The enormous round pillars of Gloucester and Tewkesbury, tall and massive, supporting rows of round arches very sparingly ornamented, with a small plain triforium above, only exist in these two solitary examples in the two great churches of the Severn Land.[*]

They have a beauty of their own, these stern and solemn Norman naves of Gloucester and Tewkesbury.[†] It is true,

---

[*] I speak, of course, of England. There are, I understood from Professor Freeman, a few rare examples on the Continent, on a smaller scale, however.

[†] The Norman nave of Gloucester "would just hold the nave of Tewkesbury, as one of a nest of boxes will hold the next in size, leaving no space between the outside walls of the smaller and the inside walls of the larger church."—Blunt, ' Tewkesbury Abbey."

they possess not the rich grace of Durham and Peterborough, the most perfect forms of Norman church-work; but the vast pillars supporting the round and massive arches impress the beholder in a way which Durham and Peterborough, with all their marvellous beauty and winning charm, fail to do. They give an idea of strength, permanence, power, which no other buildings seem capable of suggesting. Historically viewed, they are splendid types of that magnificent Norman race which designed them and built them up an enduring work—a work which, after nearly eight hundred years, is as fresh and strong as it was on the day when the master-builder laid the last stone on the completed piers.

Both Gloucester and Tewkesbury, with their vast naves divided from the aisles by those tall and massive cylindrical pillars, suffer greatly from the loss of the original roof. As it is at present in Tewkesbury—and Gloucester is not very dissimilar—the roof is stone, but the vaulting is too low and does not harmonize well with the vast columnar piers beneath. This stone vaulting was the work of the fourteenth or the end of the thirteenth century. The original Norman roof of both Gloucester and Tewkesbury was no doubt in the first instance flat, like that now existing at Peterborough, more or less coloured, and was of wood. In both instances these wooden roofs were destroyed by a desolating fire. There is scarcely an example of a Norman abbey or cathedral which has not in very early days severely suffered from fire. The original wooden roofs could of course be destroyed, while the stone walls and mighty Norman pillars and piers would suffer comparatively little damage. In Gloucester the great columns preserve to this day the red stains of fire; probably the burning rafters from the roof fell upon them. These constant and repeated fires were no doubt the result of imperfect and careless lighting—a lighting constantly required in the late afternoon and night services prescribed by the Benedictine use.

*Nave of Tewkesbury Abbey*

When brilliantly lit for the
evening services these vast Nor-
man naves lose their cold aspect, and are indescribably
beautiful and solemn ; but by daylight, although most grave and
impressive, they leave a sense of coldness. The colour of the
stained windows somewhat relieves this feeling of deathly chill.
In pre-Reformation days the altar of the Holy Rood, blazing
with its gorgeous ornaments in front of the choir screen and
rood loft, the many side altars, each a wealth of colour and of
gold, a free use of bright colouring, varied with gilding on the
flat wooden or on the vaulted ceiling, and on portions, at least,

of the tall columns themselves, would, without detracting aught from the harmonious proportions of the building, have supplied that tone of warmth and colour which is now so sadly lacking.

What in the sister abbey of Gloucester, where the choir is very large and with a roof elevated far above that of the nave, would be a hazardous proceeding,* in Tewkesbury the modern restorers have carried out, perhaps to the advantage of the great church: namely, they have swept away all vestige of the rood screen, or choir screen, and thrown the whole church virtually open from east to west.† But the choir of Tewkesbury is comparatively small, and its roof does not, like the Gloucester choir roof, soar above the nave. The effect on the general view from all points in the nave of Tewkesbury is very beautiful. The choir, which in its restored state possesses a considerable amount of gold and colour, forms an exquisite termination to the vista, and with its carved and gilded roof and crowd of chauntries and tombs, rich in curious tracery and crowned with carved pinnacles, with the gorgeous jewelled windows of the De Clares lighting up the sanctuary and its tombs with a charmed light, satisfies the eye with a very confusion of mysterious beauty and delicate colour.

The central tower of Tewkesbury has been well and truthfully described as perhaps one of the grandest that was

---

* This sweeping away of the original division between nave and choir—the rood screen or choir screen—and thus completely changing the original design of the great Benedictine architects, is nearly always a perilous experiment, fraught with the gravest danger, to go no further, to the acoustic properties of the building. Where the choir is comparatively small, as at Tewkesbury, and even at Hereford, the effect, perhaps, is pleasing to some ; but can this be alleged as the case in Worcester ? How gladly would many see the screen restored there ! I could cite other well-known instances of these doubtful "improvements" carried out by modern restorers in the work of the great masters in architecture of the eleventh and two following centuries.

† Since this was written a light screen with carved open work has been placed on the site of the old massive screen of the Benedictine architect ; it is, however, so delicately light that it scarcely obstructs the view of the choir.

ever designed in the Romanesque period. It is now 132 feet high and 46 feet square, and, for an Early Norman tower, extraordinarily rich in decoration, the ornamental work consisting of arcades and round-headed windows, with the chevron or zigzag ornament used profusely.

No doubt this tower formed part of the original plan of Fitz-Hamon's architect, and was built about A.D. 1140. It was originally capped with a lofty spire of timber, probably covered with lead. The spire stood for several hundred years; it fell while service was going on in the abbey A.D. 1559. It is not improbable that this ruin, occasioned by a storm, was partly owing to some neglect consequent upon the poverty and confusion succeeding the Dissolution. "These wooden spires are common, and, though probably few are now in existence coeval with the towers, there is no reason to suppose that they have not been reproduced with tolerable accuracy. There is one at Bocherville, and a similar finish is known to have belonged to the tower of Tewkesbury, but it was blown down by a storm in the sixteenth century."[*] The twin towers at the west end of Durham Cathedral in some respects resemble the noble Norman tower of our abbey. The only modern addition to this tower is the embattled parapet and the four pinnacles which crown the work. These were built as late as A.D. 1660. Though they are not strictly in character with the architecture, they harmonize fairly well with the building, and cannot be termed a disfigurement.

After the Norman tower, which on the whole may be said to be unrivalled, the most remarkable exterior feature in the abbey is the curious and striking west front. This is almost wholly taken up with one enormous but beautiful arch, which is in its composition simply unique. A vast semicircular arch, recessed in six orders supported by lofty shafts, occupies

[*] Mr. Petit, "Tewkesbury Abbey Church," *Trans. Gl. and Bristol Arch. Soc.*, vol. v., part 1.

R

the central compartment. The recess is sixty-five feet high
and thirty-four feet wide. The space of the arch is now
filled with a large window, put in towards the end of the
seventeenth century in place of one destroyed by a storm.

It has been suggested with some probability that the old
Norman arrangement comprised several smaller windows
within the great arch, and that these were superseded in the
fourteenth century, when the great alterations were made in
the choir. This is almost certain, for the love of stained glass
in the fourteenth and fifteenth centuries had reached such a pitch
that we find many churches of that date literally with walls
nearly all " window." The magnificent east end of Gloucester
—literally composed of superb stained glass—is a most conspicuous instance of this fashion. The date of the Gloucester
window is as early as A.D. 1340—1350. The Tewkesbury
west window would not be many years later. But, alas ! here,
different to the matchless Gloucester east window, the old
glass has all disappeared.

A friendly but true critic writes of this striking west front
thus :—" The western front, fine as it is, has degenerated
greatly from the original design of the Norman architect (this
original design cannot even be guessed). As this noble arch
stands at present, it is extremely beautiful in itself, but it has
an incomplete appearance, seeming to want a *raison d'être*
and being too large a jewel for its setting." Possibly western
towers were originally contemplated. Some rough Norman
masonry has been detected in the south clerestory which has
suggested this. If such were the plan of Fitz-Hamon's architect, the great solitary Norman arch, which now really consti-
tutes the west front, would have received a mass of support on
either side.

But while Tewkesbury Abbey possesses possibly the
noblest Norman tower still existing, and still presents with but

*Teakesbury Abbey, from the south-west.*

little change—save in its ornamentation at the east end—the
primitive Norman arrangement of a great church built in the
first years of the twelfth century, its chief glory after all
consists in the beautiful tombs and exquisite chapels and
chauntries grouped round the choir, some of them sadly
defaced it is true, but still lovely in their ruined condition—
tombs and chauntries erected by different members of that
famous house who were lords and patrons of the abbey and
the adjacent lands from the first year of William Rufus until
far on in the reign of Edward IV. For nearly four centuries,
the lineal descendants, either in the male or female line, of
Fitz-Hamon, lord of the honour of Gloucester, the founder
of the famous abbey, without a single break succeeded each
other under the famous names of De Clare, Despenser, and
Beauchamp, until Isabella, the King-maker's daughter, wife of
the Duke of Clarence, the last Lady of Tewkesbury, was laid
to sleep in the vault behind the high altar of the church in the
year of grace 1477.

There has been marvellously little change in the general
appearance of the exterior of the abbey during the seven
hundred and fifty years which have passed since the Norman
mason laid the topmost stone on that massive tower which
still crowns the mighty pile. This morning through the white
mists curling round it, as they rose from their bed among
the water-meadows, it seemed a vast shadowy pile streaked
with dark purple shadows; at mid-day, when the white
wreathing mists were sun-scattered, it shone in the golden
sunshine, a pale grey silver abbey; in the eventide, when the
sun was setting behind the distant forest hills, the mosses and
lichens on the stone caught the rosy glow, and tinged the
walls and tower with the richest sunset reds.

Long years have certainly deepened the shadows and
softened the colours; but the outside of the abbey with its

lordly tower, set in the bright green water-meadows, is hardly changed since Earl Robert, Beauclerc's son, and his empress-sister looked on it, one of the few bright peaceful scenes in their war-worn life, or since Prince John, Cœur-de-Lion's brother, gazed with his shifty, troubled eyes on the same abbey, the coveted dowry of Isabel, daughter and heiress of William Fitzcount, Earl of Gloucester, the wife of John's early years.

But within considerable change has passed over the great church of Fitz-Hamon. The nave, with its massive columnar piers, save in its roof, has not been touched; but the choir is very different from the choir built by the Norman earls who claimed near kindred with the Conqueror and the early Plantagenet kings.

Here again in Tewkesbury the story of the sister abbey of Gloucester is repeated. It was in the latter end of the thirteenth and in the first half of the fourteenth century, that the monk-artists—and there were not a few artists hidden under the shadow of the Benedictine hoods—began to grow impatient of the stern plainness * of the Norman school of architecture; lighter and seemingly more graceful forms of tracery and of arch had been brought back by successive bands of crusaders from the lands of the East. They were weary too of the dark and sombre interiors, scarcely lit with the small round-arch windows which Gundulph and William of Carileph built into the walls of Rochester and Durham, and Herbert of Losinga and Serlo into the lordly piles of Norwich and Gloucester; so the monks of Gloucester and Tewkesbury determined to change the dark massive Norman choirs into something richer and more aery and graceful. The mighty strides, too, which the craft of artists in stained glass had lately made, seemed also to call for new and vaster windows,

---

* I have discussed some of the reasons of the impatience in " Dreamland in History."

the better to display the newly-discovered marvels of exquisite transparent colouring.

But although the architecture and decoration of the choirs of the sister abbeys were changed from Norman to Gothic somewhere about the same period, the wrko in the two choirs is very different in character and execution.

In Gloucester the monk-builders brought about the change, by flinging, as it were, over the massive Norman pillars and round arches a white stone veil of Gothic tracery. They simply cut away the stone where it was necessary, and fixed the new work on the old; the Gothic work may really be said to be "veneered" on the old Norman. The Gloucester changes were besides far more elaborate than those of Tewkesbury, for they—the monks of Gloucester—ambitious of possessing a soaring choir, raised the vast eastern limb of their abbey far above its old height, and satisfied the craving for more light by building at the east end a sumptuous wall of rich tracery for the new jewelled glass—a very wall of crystal it now seems, gleaming with deep dark reds and the tenderest blues on a ground of an inimitable silvery white.

In Gloucester too, probably suggested by the necessities of their peculiar way of ornamenting the round Norman pillars, the monk-architect invented that perfectly new school of Gothic subsequently called Perpendicular, the long straight lines of tracery lying more easily over the great circular pillars and round arches. In Tewkesbury—where all the choir above the capitals of the lower piers was destroyed to make way for the new work—the Gothic is pure Decorated. The monk-builder there had no reason for devising a fresh form. There is scarcely any Perpendicular in this albey, save here and there in a bit of later work. The feeling and character of the lovely choir of Tewkesbury are Decorated, while in Gloucester they are Perpendicu'ar.

Round the old Norman choir of Tewkesbury was constructed a crown of seven chapels. In Gloucester there are fourteen chapels grouped round the east end, including the choir, triforium, and crypt. In Westminster there is a similar "crown." Ruskin, in "The Bible of Amiens," in his own quaint, beautiful fashion, gives us the reason why the sacred architects of the great building centuries loved to wreathe this "coronet" of chapels round the choir. "From the aisles surrounding the choir branched off a series of radiating chapels, each dedicated to some separate saint. This conception of the Company of Christ with His Saints (the eastern chapel of all being the Virgin's) was at the root of the entire disposition of the apse, with its supporting and dividing buttresses and piers ; and the architectural form can never be well delighted in, unless in some sympathy with the spiritual imagination out of which it rose. We talk foolishly and feebly of symbols and types ; in old Christian architecture every part is literal. The cathedral is for its builders the house of God ; it is surrounded, like an earthly king's, with minor lodgings for the servants." These Tewkesbury chapels were entirely rebuilt by the fourteenth-century architect. The Gothic of these was Decorated—like the choir—but the tracery of the windows is almost flamboyant.

During most of this fourteenth century, the famous Despenser family were lords of Tewkesbury and patrons of the abbey— Hugh Despenser the younger, the ill-fated friend of King Edward II., being created Earl of Gloucester on his marrying Eleanor, the heiress of the De Clares, A.D. 1321. It was under the Despensers that the choir of Tewkesbury put on its present beautiful robe of stone. It was the same house that inserted in the seven splendid windows of the choir that magnificent jewelled glass which even now—alas ! somewhat broken and defaced —is still one of the glories of the noble abbey.

# CHAPTER VI.

IT was this same fourteenth century too which saw the building
of the well-known group of chauntries and sepulchral monuments which encircle the abbey choir.* The earliest of these,
evidently in former days a tomb of rare beauty, near the
high altar at the back of the once splendid but now broken
and defaced sedilia, contained, probably in the *loculus* † still
visible, the mutilated remains of Hugh le Despenser the
younger, put to death and then quartered at Hereford, by
order of Queen Isabella, as a guerdon for his loyalty to her
husband, the poor dethroned Edward II. This must have
been a superb monument. There are niches for forty statues,
which have all now disappeared, and the whole was once richly
coloured and gilded.

On the north side of the altar there is one of the stateliest
tombs in England, with the effigies of a knight and lady
beneath the graceful canopy. The knight is " Hugo Tertius

---

* With one exception ; the Beauchamp Chauntry was erected early in the
following century, a few years later, about 1422.

† These poor remains, unembalmed, no doubt soon perished, and the
*loculus* was subsequently opened, and the coffin of Abbot Cotes was placed in
it. This took place, however, at a comparatively recent date.

S

le Despensere," and the lady is Elizabeth his wife, of the family of the Montacutes, Earls of Salisbury. They both lie in that touching attitude of prayer, as though wistfully waiting the angel's summons to arise—she clad in the quaint graceful dress of the ladies of the brilliant court of Edward III., he in that splendid armour, all emblazoned with the heraldic symbols of his proud house, in which the chivalry of England so often in those restless ages rode down the chivalry of France. The gold and colour, which once made this fair tomb a very dream of beauty, are gone ; only faint traces of the colour here and there remain. The features of the knightly " Despensere " are battered and mutilated, the exquisite tracery and carving grievously defaced, but even in its scarred and faded condition it is still beautiful, and recalls many a page of the story of an era of devotion and loyalty which helped not a little to make our England strong and great.

Close by this fair " Despensere " tomb rises another lofty and graceful canopy of fretted stonework, almost the exact copy of Lord Hugh's stately monument. There also, beneath the canopy, lies a knightly figure mailed and helmeted, with hands too crossed in prayer.

Mark it well. It is the effigy of the man who bore the standard of the Third Edward in many a stricken field, and always to victory.

It is Guy de Brien, who became Lord of Tewkesbury when he married the widow of Lord Hugh le Despenser, who sleeps so close beside them. Even in that age of splendid valour, De Brien was known as the bravest of the brave. History tells how on the field of battle the great English king dubbed him knight-banneret, and chose him one of the first knights of the proud Order of the Garter.

But his wife, Elizabeth de Montacute, preferred to lie beside her first love, Lord Hugh le Despenser ; so Sir Guy de Brien, lord of Welwyn and many another castle, sleeps

*Tomb of Sir Guy de Brien.*

alone, and the Lady of Tewkesbury, his wife, moulders away, a few yards distant, by the side of " Hugo Tertius," her first husband.

Across the choir, in a once gorgeous chauntry, lies another Despenser.   His effigy, quaintly kneeling amidst the fretted work wh'ch canopies this little " Trinity " chapel, as it is named, keeps in prayer, as it seems, an eternal watch and ward in his ancestral church.   Between these stately tombs, under the very altar-shadow, lie in two rows the remains of the two lines of English nobles once lords of the storied abbey. Their monuments have perished—the very brasses which once marked the spot where the remains of the Lords Despenser and Clare were laid have been rifled. Little tablets which in our own time reverent hands have let into the sacred floor just indicate the name of each great noble and the site where his coffin rests.

In the place of honour, on the immediate right of the high altar, in the last years of the same century (A.D. 1397)— the century in which so much rich and varied work in marble and stone and coloured glass was planned and executed—the abbot of the monastery built a beautiful chapel in the new style of Gothic (the Perpendicular, lately introduced at Gloucester, A.D 1327—1336) over the slab which covered the grave of Fitz-Hamon, the illustrious founder of the abbey. The body had been removed in the middle of the thirteenth century from its first resting-place in the chapter-house, the church not being finished when Fitz Hamon died. The actual tomb is sadly disfigured ; the brass has disappeared, but the tiles of the little chapel, dating from the fifteenth century, bear those arms which tradition has assigned to the great Norman —the rampant lion and the engrailed cross of the abbey. At the end of the last century the tomb was opened, and enclosed in a leaden wrapper the bones of the Conqueror's powerful warrior-kinsman were once more looked on.

But the most elaborate and striking of the splendid chauntries and sepulchral monuments which surround the choir at Tewkesbury dates from a few years later. It was the work of Isabel Despenser, the heiress of the abbey and the Tewkesbury estates, who married Richard Beauchamp, Earl of Abergavenny and Worcester. " Ricardus de Bello Campo," as the contemporary chronicle terms him, was mortally wounded by a stone shot out of a catapult at the siege of Meaux. This happened A.D. 1421. His young widowed countess, during her first years of bitter sorrow, devoted herself to adorning and beautifying the exquisite " Beauchamp " chapel, as it is usually called. Within and without, judging from even its present defaced state, it

*The Trinity Chapel.*

In the quaint canopy on the roof is a kneeling figure, representing " Edwardus Dominus le Despensere," who died A.D. 1375.

must have been once a very marvel of exquisite workmanship —above, with its elaborate canopies, it seems still a delicate lacework of stone ; beneath, with its heraldic blazonry telling of royal and illustrious ancestry of the dead past, it was evidently a maze of rich and tender colouring. Each jewelled niche, once holding its statue of saint or king; its perfect roof, beautiful with fair fan tracery ; its quaint conceits of shape and form, but all in perfect harmony, were evidently the work of one of those great monk-artists, the glory of those now

forgotten homes of prayer and thought, and marvellous and
inimitable conceptions.    Yet "souvent femme varie, bien fou
qui s'y fie!" No sooner was this marvellously lovely *in me-*
*moriam* chauntry complete, than the Lady Isabel bestowed her
hand and the broad Tewkesbury lands on another—"Ricardus
de Bello Campo," her first husband's cousin.

This Richard was known in history as the great Earl of
Warwick and Albemarle, and he played for many years a most
distinguished part in the stirring events of his age.    King
Henry V. left him guardian of his boy, Henry VI., the saintly,
unhappy Red Rose king.    Richard de Beauchamp subsequently became Regent of France   Worn out with excessive
toil and thought, he died, while still in his prime, at Rouen.
The Lady Isabel only survived him a few months.    She lies
in her beloved abbey, but her splendid tomb, of which history
speaks, has disappeared.    In the restoration works in 1875
fragments of the wooden coffin, lined with costly silk, which
held her embalmed body, were found.    The embalmed body
itself was, however, preserved, though the coffin had fallen
to pieces.    The plain linen shroud was still wrapped round
the countess; the bright auburn hair of the Lady Isabel was
as though four centuries and more had not passed away since
she was left there to sleep.    A stone slab covered the grave,
and on the *inner side* a cross was engraved and the prayer,
"Mercy, Lord Jesu."    The restorers carefully replaced the
remains and laid the great stone again upon the grave, with
its solemn prayer still towards her face.

There are other monuments—some still beautiful in their
partly ruined and defaced state, all interesting and suggestive.
Rich though Tewkesbury be in these outward proofs of our
forefathers' reverent care for the great dead, it is richer still in
memories.    For instance, no stately tomb marks the sleeping-
place of the Red Rose hope, the brave boy Prince Edward,

*The " Warwick" Chauntry.*

Erected by Lady Isabel, Countess of Warwick, in memory of her first husband.

who perished after the last deadly fight between the two
Roses, beneath the sacred abbey walls.

The body of Prince Edward of Wales was buried in the
abbey. The traditional spot is under the lantern of the
central tower. No monument seems ever to have been
raised to his memory. The fortunes of his royal house were
hopelessly ruined in the battle of Tewkesbury, and men at first
feared to honour the memory of the representative of a lost
and defeated cause, and in after years, when the bitter feuds
of the rival Roses were but a sorrowful memory, the nameless
grave at Tewkesbury and its chivalrous, unhappy occupant, the
boy Prince of Wales, were forgotten.*

* A little brass tablet has been lately let into the pavement on the traditional
spot.

Another remarkable sepulchre of men whose names were once "household words" in the history of England is on the south side of the double chapel of St. Nicholas and St. James, which opens into the ambulatory north of the choir. There the Duke of Somerset and other Lancastrian leaders of the highest rank were hastily laid after their execution in the little market-place (A.D. 1471).

One more sorrowful memory of the loved abbey must be recorded before I close the story of Tewkesbury.

After the fatal battle the lands of Warwick the King-maker, including the lordship of the abbey, were of course confiscated by the victorious Edward IV. The Tewkesbury estates were given to his brother, Duke George of Clarence, who had married Warwick's daughter, Isabel Neville.*

But the splendid heritage brought no blessing to the daughter of the dead King-maker, or to her fickle, brilliant consort, royal Clarence. All kinds of dark stories were whispered of George of Clarence. Men said the Duchess Isabel was slowly dying of poison given her by her false husband. Various motives were suggested for the deed, such as love, greed, ambition. In the infirmary of the monastery of her ancestral abbey her third child was born, but only to die. Isabel never rallied; she was taken from the infirmary of the old religious house to Warwick, where she expired a few days later. Her body was brought back to Tewkesbury, and lay in state under "a hearse" in the splendid choir. With her ancestors' stately tombs around her she was exposed for thirty-five days, and then was laid in a newly-hewn vault behind the high altar on the east side. This was on the 4th January, 1477, scarcely six years after the decisive battle beneath the abbey walls; only a few days later, "false, fleet-

* The story of the marriage and the character of George and Isabel are sketched with great power and picturesqueness in Lord Lytton's beautiful romance, "The Last of the Barons."

ing, perjured Clarence," was put to death in the Tower. The body of the duke was brought to the abbey and laid beside his wife Isabel in the new "Clarence" vault. No Gothic sculptured canopy, not even a plain marble slab, exists to mark the resting-place of the last Lady of Tewkesbury or of her faithless royal husband.

The descendants of Fitz-Hamon, the Conqueror's cousin, the trusted friend and counsellor of Rufus, had held the great Tewkesbury estates and lordship of the noble abbey which Fitz-Hamon had founded for well-nigh four centuries. Most of them slept within the sacred abbey walls, but Isabel Neville was the last* of her famous line who had to do with Tewkesbury and its great church, either in life or death.

There is little more to tell of the abbey and the noble heritage of the illustrious Norman house of De Clare, De-spenser, and Neville. After the execution of George of Clarence the estates passed into the hands of the Crown. The days, too, of the famous monastery were numbered. Its possessions, after the Dissolution, became State property.

Tewkesbury Abbey will always possess a special interest for the student of English history, as well as for the anti-quarian. During four centuries it was the centre of the life as well as the home in death of one of those powerful families whose great possessions and still greater traditions constituted one of the elements of the strength of England during her long period of struggle with the leading nations of the continent of Europe, and her slow period of growth at home. Outside the family of the royal Plantagenets—with whom on several occasions it was, however, allied in marriage —no house, perhaps, was more influential, few so mighty and

---

* Isabel Neville and George of Clarence left two children—a boy and girl. They both perished by the headsman's axe in the Tower. The boy, after a long imprisonment, was executed in 1499. The girl, afterwards known as Margaret Plantagenet, Marchioness of Salisbury, years later (A.D. 1541), was the heroine of one of the many gloomy tragedies which darkened the reign of Henry VIII.

T

powerful, as the descendants of Fitz-Hamon, lord of the honour of Gloucester. The descent from the mighty founder of the line was unbroken from the first days of Rufus till the time when Edward IV. was firmly seated on the English throne. When sons failed, a daughter and heiress of the direct line married some noble scion of another famous house, and handed on that splendid heritage of which our abbey was the centre—the abbey they were never tired of beautifying and enriching.

During their four centuries of existence few were the events of moment in the story of England in which the head of the noble house of Tewkesbury took no part. In one century the descendant of the Norman Fitz-Hamon was called De Clare, in another Despenser, in another Neville, Beauchamp, or Warwick; but under one or other of these time-honoured names, the lords of Tewkesbury for four hundred eventful years were rarely absent from the roll-call of the leading English chieftains. Rufus, the king, died in Fitz-Hamon's arms in the Malwood Chase of the New Forest. Earl Robert never left the side of his sister Maud, the empress-queen—Earl Robert, one of the truest knights that ever lived among us. Gilbert de Clare signed Magna Charta; another Gilbert fought with the patriot lords at Evesham; a third Gilbert fell in the front ranks in the field of Bannockburn. Hugh le Despenser died the cruellest of deaths for his ill-fated king and master, the second Edward. Guy de Brien of Tewkesbury carried the proud standard of Edward and of England at Cressy. In the first roll of illustrious Knights of the Garter, the great order of English chivalry, we read the name of Edward Despenser. When the victor of Agincourt died only too soon, Warwick of Tewkesbury was left the guardian of his little son, the heir of France and England. This same Warwick became Regent of France. Another Warwick, lord of the abbey, is known in the history of the two

Roses wars as "King-maker" and "last of the Barons." When the vault behind the altar—the nameless vault—was closed upon the King-maker's daughter Isabella and her husband, the false Duke of Clarence, the last page of the long and eventful story of the great abbey had been written.

IN a remote corner of Worcestershire, between the green uplands of the Cotswold range and the solitary Bredon Hill, there is a broad lawn-like meadow falling somewhat sharply on the east side towards the storied Avon, which as a silver fringe seems to border the grassy slope. Immediately on the left is a lofty tower rich with graceful tracery and sculptured fancies, tenderly coloured with those soft grey hues which only centuries of storm and sunshine can paint upon white walls; on the right runs a long irregular ruined wall, uncared for and unbeautiful save for the grey-green moss and lichens which partly veil its broken stones.

The stranger who knew nothing of its story would surely smile if he were told that beneath the grass and daisies round him were hidden the vast foundation stories of one of the mightiest of our proud mediæval abbeys; that on the very spot where he was standing were once grouped a forest of tall columns bearing up lofty fretted roofs; that all around once

The Bell Tower
Evesham.

were altars brilliant with colour and with gold; that besides
the many altars were once grouped on that sacred spot chauntries and tombs, many of them marvels of grace and beauty,
placed there in memory of men great in the service of Church
and State—of men whose names were household words in
the England of our fathers; that close by him were once
stately cloisters, great monastic buildings, including refectory,
dormitories, chapter-house, chapels, infirmary, granaries, kitchens—all the varied piles of buildings which used to make
up the hive of a great monastery.

That green meadow fringed by the Avon stream, with its solitary tower and ruined wall, is indeed the scene of a long and eventful story—a story which reaches back well-nigh a thousand years.

When central and western England were slowly emerging from the mists of confusion that covered them for more than a century after the ruin of the short-lived British rule which succeeded the departure of the Roman military colonists, the Avon-washed meadow of our story was part of the forest-land which stretched from the Cotswold range to the Severn banks. In the forest in those far-back days a swineherd named Eoves, in the service of Ecgwin, one of the earliest Mercian bishops —so runs the old legend—saw a vision of a woman in the midst of a shining cloud of glory. The swineherd related the strange sight to his master. The same appearance was vouchsafed to Ecgwin. The bishop recognised in the vision the Blessed Virgin Mary, and determined to erect on the hallowed spot a church and home of prayer. This was the beginning of the famous holy house of Evesham—" Eovesholm "—named after the poor swineherd whose eyes had been allowed to gaze on the radiant vision of Mary. The date of the vision and subsequent building of the church and monastery was in the early part of the eighth century.

A picturesque sketch of the vision of Eoves and Ecgwin has lately been painted by a friend of mine. " It was probably in the year 702," he writes, " that a strange rumour travelled through the forest of Arden to the walled stronghold of Wigornia (Worcester), where it reached the ears of Ecgwin, the third bishop of the Mercian see. It was told with much wonderment how Eoves, one of the swineherds, while wandering through a glade on the edge of the forest at Hethomme, had seen three beautiful women, who came towards him singing a sweet, unearthly song. The fact alone is recorded, not the marvelling of the foresters of Arden.

Bishop Ecgwin visited the spot where the three fair women had disappeared. Alone in the first glimmer of sunrise he beheld the Virgin Mother and her heavenly handmaidens: 'our Lady' more white-shining than lilies, says the old chronicle, more freshly sprung than roses; a ravishing fragrance filled the woods; and in one hand she carried a book, and in the other a cross beaming with golden light. Stretching forth the cross, she blessed the bishop and vanished away.

"Glad at heart, therefore, was the holy man on account of these things. He understood it to be the Divine will that this very spot should be set aside for the worship of God, and consecrated to His blessed Mother for the propitiation of the ages. Straightway a fair abbey sprang up in the forest glade. The ancient name of the place, Hethomme, fell speedily into disuse, and in the rustic speech, as the seal of the great house still testifies, the place was called Eovesholm, Evesham, after the poor swineherd Eoves.

"One wonders what Eoves himself thought of the matter; whether a kindlier fortune brightened his old age; whether he fared the less meagrely or slept the warmer as the monkish axes cleared away the centuried oaks and elms, and the beautiful work rose beside the pleasant Avon stream; whether he left children to tell of his vision and make grim comment on the growing splendour of the abbey; in a word—one wonders what Eoves thought of it all, and what was his fate."

The fortunes of Bishop Ecgwin's foundation at Evesham for several hundred years vary but little from those of Gloucester, Pershore, and a number of other more or less renowned religious houses in the Mercian kingdom. The monastery of Evesham was subject now and again to Danish depredation; then by the help of pious Mercian princes and nobles again restored and renovated, it proceeded with its quiet beneficent work of teaching and prayer, of almsgiving and ceaseless hospitality.

In some periods it was the exclusive home of monks, in others the abode of a college of seculars, of canons or uncloistered ecclesiastics, until the days of Dunstan (tenth century), when the long rivalry was decided generally throughout Saxon England in favour of the monks.

From the days of the old Mercian kings the house of Evesham was rich; successive Mercian kings endowed it with fresh grants of land. Their example was followed by their greater successors who ruled as over-kings in England.

*Seal of Evesham Abbey (obverse).*

Domesday Book tells us that in the days of King Edward the Confessor, Evesham possessed in central and western England some 33,000 acres. After Hastings the Abbot Aegilwyn was one of the few great Saxon ecclesiastics who retained the confidence of the Conqueror William.

In the unhappy winter of A.D. 1070, the year that made the Conqueror king over the whole land, one hundred thousand human beings are said to have died of cold and hunger; this was the terrible outcome of the Norman harrying of Derbyshire and the North Midlands.

In this season of dire misery, the Abbey of Evesham,

then ruled by Abbot Aegilwyn, was conspicuous in its efforts
to relieve the awful suffering. During the dreary winter
season many a man of high rank, driven by the Normans
from the land and home of his fathers, found shelter and help
in the holy house of St. Ecgwin.

Men say how in that gloomy year the houses, the streets,
the very churchyard of Evesham, were crowded with sufferers
dying of cold and hunger. The Evesham Chronicle tells us
how the tender-hearted Dominus Abbas gave orders that

*Seal of Evesham Abbey (reverse).*

the stricken wanderers should be lovingly cared for; from
his own table he fed daily thirty of these hollow-eyed
strangers, himself washing the feet of twelve others, and never
shrinking from the unhappy lepers among them.

Aegilwyn's successor, the Norman Walter, chaplain to Lanfranc, a monk of Duke Robert of Normandy's Abbey of
Cerasia, was appointed by the Conqueror himself, and preserved
the abbey and its possessions by the cession of a third of its
great estates to Odo, Bishop of Bayeux and Earl of Kent, the
Conqueror's half-brother, and Urse d'Abitot, the well-known
sheriff of Worcestershire.

U

Eleven years after Hastings, like so many of the great French ecclesiastics who received abbeys at the hands of the Conqueror, Abbot Walter determined to rebuild the abbey church of his house in a style befitting the important position of Evesham. It was a wonderful moment to obtain contributions to such a work. Many of the Normans were dismayed at the sight of the woe and misery in the Anglo-Saxon land, the first visible result of their great conquest, and were ready and willing to lavish gold and treasure for the building of what were looked on as "abbeys of expiation" by not a few in those days of ruthless deeds, followed after by swift and sharp remorse. The building of the new Norman abbey went on rapidly; much of the crypt and the great eastern limb of the new church was completed before the passing away of William the Conqueror.

The work was costly, and the income of the abbey lands did not nearly suffice for this new effort. A strange expedient was devised; the same writer, quoted above, thus graphically describes it:—" What was to be done? Our Dominus Abbas was not at a loss. He summoned to him two wise monks who had travelled through many distant shires, and confided to them his project. They assented; and so with cross and burning tapers, accompanied some distance on their way by the brotherhood singing their rhymed Latin canticles, the two set forth with a small train, and in the midst a horse bearing the shrine of St. Ecgwin. Picture, if you can, that strange little band of cowled figures traversing the wild England of those days; now lost in the depths of the forest; now moving along some old Roman road, rendered here and there almost impassable by swamp and quagmire; now passing hurriedly through the charred ruins of some townstead ravaged by the Normans; now pausing at some monastery gate, crossing some dangerous river-ford, or making a brief sojourn in some busy town to preach, to exhibit the shrine of the saint,

to let the diseased and suffering touch some miraculous relic, and to gather such offerings as the piety or gratitude or super-stition of the people prompted them to make. Many a coin and trinket found their way into the satchels of Hereman and his companions."

The massive Norman work went on in the nave and tower and mighty transepts during the next hundred years. Vast buildings were added to the already existing religious house, chapels, refectory, dormitories, abbot's lodgings, chapter-house, kitchens, stables—all the many dependencies of a great Benedictine monastery. But the abbey was the loved centre of the whole ; successive abbots added to its splendour and stately appearance. As in the case of Gloucester and other similar great Norman monasteries, graceful and costly decora-tive work was gradually added to the stern, grave designs of Abbot Walter and the eleventh-century builders. In the fourteenth century much of the old work was recast, and a noble central tower was completed. But all this has disappeared. The very foundation stories of the great abbey, massive and vast though they must have been, are hidden under the green meadow washed by the Avon. One ruined arch is really all that remains of past magnificence, and antiquaries only dare to guess at the original use and position even of this one melancholy and solitary relique of a vanished city of God.

From the time of the Conquest until the days of the Reformation, from William I. to Henry VIII., a period of well-nigh five hundred years, Evesham Abbey and the great Benedictine house beneath its shadow occupied a foremost position among the great religious homes of England. Nor by any means did it date the beginnings of its high position and influence to Norman William and his famous minister of religion, Lanfranc ; for centuries before the Conquest Eve-sham had ranked among the chiefest of the Anglo-Saxon houses of prayer. It had undergone many changes and had endured various fortunes, but the unerring record of Domes-day tells us that this great house, far from owing its high position to the Norman Conquest, rather suffered in its fortunes after the arrival of the French strangers. In some respects it was even a typical religious house, for it owed its far-reaching influence to no powerful family like Tewkesbury, to no court favour like royal Gloucester, so often in Saxon and Norman times the residence of the kings of England. It was simply one of those monasteries in a purely rural district which during so many storm-filled years educated, comforted, helped in a thousand ways all classes and orders of the commonwealth.

In its palmy days the interior of our famous abbey must have been inexpressibly solemn and imposing. It was beautiful with the strange rich beauty of splendid symbolism in times when a great church like Evesham was the sculptured and coloured text-book of Christianity. We read of the grand Norman nave of eight bays, the crossing of the same date, the aisleless transept, the delicate Early English presbytery of five bays, square-ended and without a projecting Lady chapel—but all enriched with Perpendicular additions.

A writer some 250 years ago* tells us that at Evesham " the abbey and cloisters were of curious workmanship, and had withinside one hundred and sixty-four gilt marble pillars. There were also in the church sixteen altars, all in so many chapels dedicated to their respective saints."

But the story of Evesham would never have risen in interest above the story of other abbeys—the equals of Evesham in wealth and influence, equals too in the grandeur of their stately churches, and in the magnitude and beauty of the surrounding buildings—had not Evesham been the closing scene of a mighty struggle, the effects of which have left a lasting impress upon English history ; had not the vanished abbey

* Habyngdon—*temp.* Charles I.

*Seal of Simon de Montfort.*

been the grave of the far-seeing chieftain of the struggle who passed away, as many another great one has passed away, amid defeat and seeming failure.

Inseparably connected with Evesham and its famous abbey is the memory of Simon de Montfort, Earl of Leicester. To the vast majority of his countrymen De Montfort is now but the shadow of a great name, who in the reign of King Henry III., in a bloody death on the stricken field received the well-earned guerdon of his rebellion ; but he was no ordinary rebel.

De Montfort, who had become a true Englishman, dreamed of an England very different from the country which Henry III. misgoverned, and for a time he succeeded in creating a great party composed of barons, clergy, and private citizens sharing his views. In his far-seeing mind the elements of the popular government which has assisted so largely in making the England of to-day were first thought out.

By birth a Frenchman and heir to the proud traditions of the house which had won for itself the position of sovereign lords in the south of France, and the reputation of being the successful defenders of what was then reputed as orthodoxy, Simon in early life, as heir through his grandmother to the Leicester estates, had elected to become an English subject, and in time won the love and the hand of Princess Eleanor, daughter of King John, sister of Henry III. His royal marriage, his famous name, his vast estates, and, chief of all, his splendid abilities as a statesman and general, won him in time the acknowledged supremacy among the foremost English nobles.

It was a critical period in the story of England. The king, Henry III., utterly failed to understand the temper of the country which had wrung Magna Charta from his father. He aimed at establishing a despotism in England, and regarded the mighty country over which he ruled as an estate which should provide the materials for a splendid and luxurious life for himself and his favourites, who were mostly chosen from foreign houses.

For a brief season De Montfort was master of the destinies of the country, and his chief work was the summoning of a Parliament in which *representatives of the towns* were called upon for the first time to share in the national deliberations.

This momentous change in the constitution—a change which has since worked with such far-reaching effect in the great English story—was Simon de Montfort's real title to honour. The author of this new departure in government soon perished, jealousies in the powerful faction he had called into being rapidly undermined his influence, and the royal party was after a brief interval enabled to meet him in the field and to crush his divided forces. De Montfort fell, and his name was branded as a traitor's. But his great thought has never perished, and from his time onwards the towns and cities of England have always shared with an ever-increasing influence in the government of the country—have with ever-growing power held the balance between the disorderly and often selfish rule of the barons and the unchecked despotism

of the Crown. Simon de Montfort may justly be regarded
as the real founder of the House of Commons.

The scene of the fatal battle in which this patriot statesman lost his life was on the abbey lands. Evesham, in
the neighbourhood of his famous castle and broad estates,
was well known and loved by Simon. It was the "Mother
Church" of his vast possessions. It was within its sacred walls
that Simon lodged the night before the battle. It was from
the tall abbey tower that his watchmen saw the royal banners of
Prince Edward's host approach. It was within the holy precincts that he made his dispositions for the fatal battle. It was
from its gates that he rode forth for the last time. De Montfort again entered the abbey, it is true, but it was as a
disfigured corpse, to be laid to rest before the high altar of
the storied pile. For a long period the tomb of Earl De
Montfort was the object of popular pilgrimage. Thousands
have knelt at the grave of the patriot earl. That hallowed
sepulchre, and the memories which clustered thickly round it,

have served to raise the vanished abbey to the peculiar position which it occupied among the crowd of abbeys and religious houses then so plentifully scattered over England.

Was Simon de Montfort after all a patriot hero, or a turbulent traitor baron ? *Væ victis*—the Muse of History has no respect for the unfortunate! His memory, like his mutilated corpse, has been often treated with scant honour. But surely he was no ordinary rebel ; his work has been strangely enduring, and has contributed not a little to the matchless fortunes of his adopted country. Still those who admire him most, mourn least over the rout of Evesham and the death of the warrior-statesman. His temper and disposition ill fitted him for over-much prosperity. Had he been victor in the contest it is hard to imagine what line of conduct he would have pursued. He would have been too powerful to have lived on the steps of the throne. Perhaps, fortunately for the weal of England, he was encountered by a prince who became the greatest king (he was Edward I.) that ever ruled over her. Prince Edward, who met De Montfort and routed him in the bloody Evesham field, had ever been the friend — to some extent he ever remained the pupil— of De Montfort. It was from De Montfort that Edward learnt the art of war. It was the same great master who showed the future king " what was to be done for England, and the spirit in which only the work could be accomplished." *

The victors in the fight of Evesham—with that savage vindictive spirit of the old Pagan Norsemen which lived still in the children of the Norman and the Anglo-Saxon, and which was only veiled with the coat-armour of mediæval chivalry—cruelly mutilated the body of the vanquished De Montfort. The head was severed from the trunk and the hands were cut off. The body, thus disfigured, was given over

* Bishop Creighton : "Simon de Montfort."

A view in the God's Acre of the vanished Abbey.

to the Evesham Abbey monks, who buried him before the high altar of their noble church. The head and hands, cruel trophies of the bloody victory, were sent to Lady Mortimer, his relentless foe, at Wigmore.

Very soon legends of their dead champion began to be woven round the people's firesides. The messenger—so runs one popular story—who bore the poor mutilated hands sewn up in a cloth, found Lady Mortimer at mass in the abbey hard by Wigmore Castle. He whispered to the lady the glad news of the Evesham fight, pointing to his awful trophy. At that moment the priest was elevating the Host; as the bystanders gazed, the hands all bloody were seen to clasp themselves as though in prayer above the messenger's head ; terrified and appalled at the dread sign, Lady Mortimer sent back the hands to Evesham Abbey, still sewn up in the blood-stained cloth which apparently they had never left.

The tomb of Simon de Montfort in its fresh glory of gold and colour was the scene of many a passionate prayer, and of not a few miracles of healing ; so runs the legend, which tells of no fewer than two hundred and thirteen miracles said to have been worked at the shrine in the abbey, and by the side of the spring on the hillside where the earl is believed to have fallen in the battle. The tomb of De Montfort in the abbey of Evesham has been compared to that of à Becket at Canterbury in the previous century, as a famous centre to which the sick and ailing resorted from all parts of England.

The sufferers would kneel and pray at the shrine of the great earl, and would bind round their foreheads "a fillet which had measured his remains" (*ad comitem Simonem mensuratus* is the phrase usually employed in the MSS.). He was even invoked, and received a kind of worship from his countrymen, who flocked in numbers to the tomb in the abbey, and kneeling there prayed to their dead patriot saint. A litany was composed in his honour, and hymns were sung in his praise.   One of them began thus:—

> " Salve Simon Montis Fortis
> Totius flos militiæ
> Duras pœnas passus mortis
> Protector gentis Angliæ."*

This devotion to Simon de Montfort in the Abbey of Evesham has a curious parallel some sixty years later in the Benedictine house of Gloucester, only Gloucester Abbey held in its favourite shrine a very different saint in the person of King Edward II., the unhappy son of Earl Simon's conqueror.

It is singular that both the neighbouring abbeys of Evesham and Gloucester owe much of their fame to the cult of the dead which so strangely sprang up in their minsters after the violent deaths of Earl Simon de Montfort and King Edward II.   The monks of Gloucester profited largely by the rich gifts offered at their shrine.   At Evesham the pilgrims were probably more numerous than even those at Gloucester, but they were of a different order in the social scale ; the Evesham pilgrims were too poor to offer costly offerings.   The lovers and mourners of Simon were the people.

This veneration is abundantly testified to by remains which we still possess of the folklore of that period.   The following is a specimen of the songs of the people in honour of the loved earl :—

> " Chanter m'estoit, mon cuer le voit, en un dure langage
> Tut en pleurant fut fat le chaunt de nostre duz baronage
> Que pur la pees, si loynz après se lesserent detrere
> Lur cors trenchers, e demembrer, pur salver Engleterre;
> Ore est ocys la flur de pris, que taunt savoit de guere
> Ly quens Montfort, sa dure mort molt emplora la terre.
>
> Mès par sa mort, le cuens Montfort conquist la victoire
> Come ly martyr de Caunterbyr, finist sa vie :
> Ne voleit pas li bon Thomas qe perist seinte Eglise
> Ly cuens auxi se combatit, e mourust saunz feyntise." *

---

* Quoted by Bishop Creighton : " Simon de Montfort."

The stranger, as he stands on the green meadow which slopes down to the bright Avon waters near the noble tower of the last abbot* is pressing hallowed ground. He is on the site of the desecrated ruined choir of the vanished abbey. Beneath his feet moulder the remains of many a great church-man. of many a mighty baron, whose names once rang through England.

* I cannot bring myself to call "Abbot of Evesham" the time-serving man who sleeps in Worcester under the style and title of dean of that great minster ; he only took up the abbot's mitre and staff to resign them to King Henry VIII. in exchange for a deanery.

And among the graves hidden in that broad green field where the daisy·starred grass veils the mighty foundation-stories of the once glorious abbey church, is, perhaps, one hidden gravestone which once bore the knightly effigy of Simon de Montfort, rebel and traitor according to the chronicles, but canonized as martyr, patriot, saint in the hearts of thousands of grateful Englishmen.

The abbey and religious house of Evesham, remote from any great highway, and at a considerable distance from important cities such as Gloucester and Worcester, during the many centuries of its existence—save for the remarkable episode of Simon de Montfort—played but little part in the story of England.

With this memorable exception, the story of the monastery of Evesham with its stately abbey was an uneventful one. Its chronicles told of long periods of self-renunciation, of brave devout life—told too of brief periods of disunion, of internal strife, of greed and self-seeking, but on the whole of duties well and bravely done ; of many a young bright life trained there to take its part in the fever and stress of the world of the day. Evesham during the long period of its existence, in common with the larger proportion of English monasteries, was on the whole occupied by men who lived simple, God-fearing lives, according to the rule prescribed to them, doing their useful task of educating the young entrusted to their care, industriously keeping alive the torch of learning, zealously ministering to the poor by whom they were surrounded. Like so many of its sister houses it was for ages a very well-spring of learning, of thought, of personal religion—a home and school of art, and, highest far of all, a home and school of prayer—of prayer constant and unremitting. What would England during those rough wild Norman and Plantagenet days have been without Evesham and its sister sacred houses of consecrated work and worship ?

The end came at last—the necessary end; the times changed. The invention of printing, and the general diffusion of knowledge consequent on the great invention, took out of the hands of the monk-dwellers in these houses of prayer one of their chief occupations. The monastery ceased to be the only or even the principal library and school. In England especially there was another cause at work which not a little contributed to the final ruin of the monastic orders. Gradually from the time of the great Edward the monastic houses of England began to separate themselves from the national life.

Once the monastic institutions with us had been strongholds of patriotism; as time went on they became more and more alienated from the national religious organization and from national feeling. In their longing to be independent of all episcopal and State control they looked to the Pope for protection, and thus they became too often instruments of a foreign power, "colonies," as it has been well said, "of Roman partisans," and so they fell. We dare not regret the great Revolution of the sixteenth century, but we may deplore the bitter accompanying circumstances. As was the case with so many of the innocent dwellers in the religious houses ruthlessly destroyed, the fair and candid historian can find no grave fault with the monks of Evesham, can advance no plea for the wanton destruction which was the sad fate of their holy house and its glorious abbey.*

Only a few words will be necessary to describe the last sad scene of havoc.

When the suppression of Evesham had been decided on, the then abbot—one Clement Lichfield—a man evidently of sincere piety and passionately devoted to his great church

---

* There is no trace of the old abbey. The solitary ruined arch at some distance from the site of the church is supposed, to have belonged to the chapter-house. The "Bell Tower," still standing, was erected in the sixteenth century, just before the Dissolution. It never formed part of the abbey church.

Ruined Arch to Chapter House.

and religious house, was compelled to resign his crozier. The
abbey was formally surrendered in the November of 1539.
During the next three years the work of destruction was

rapidly proceeded with; church, cloister, chapter-house, library and monastery were dismantled and partially taken down; Mr., afterwards Sir Philip, Hoby—a favourite of King Henry VIII.—became the purchaser from the Crown, for a comparatively small sum, of the abbey land and property, and the vast dismantled buildings in which the abbey was included were rented as a quarry for stone. More than a hundred years later—according to the borough records of 1667— the stone of the ruins of the once famous monastery appears not to have been entirely worked out.

In the words of one of the chroniclers of the fortunes of our abbey: " These buildings of the noble church and the monastery grouped around it became a quarry in the hands of lessees who did not prosper by their sacrilege, the very site a waste, and only the antiquary with mattock and lynx-eyed experience can read the little which is left of what was once a glorious house of God, and a triumph of architectural art."

# OSRIC. KING OF NORTHUMBRIA.

In the place of honour—the spot in our storied minsters usually reserved as the resting-place of the founder of the house—on the right hand of the old high altar of Gloucester Cathedral, is a stately canopied tomb. Many times during the last few years I have wandered through the glorious abbey of which, to use Mr. Ruskin's term, I have the honour of being the chief custode — now alone, now with a goodly group of companions anxious to learn something of the great book of stone men call a cathedral ; companions drawn from all sorts and conditions of men, from ministers of state, bishops and judges, down to bright, intelligent, God-fearing artisans from mighty hives of toil and industry like Birmingham and Bristol ; and as we passed through the venerable pile, every aisle, every chapel and chauntry, with its legend, with its tomb, with its jewelled window, with its half-worn picture tiles, fair pages in stone and in glass of the history of England during the last thousand years, I would stay and point to the founder's place hard by the high altar, where—slightly to alter the lines in "Marmion"—

> "A tomb with Gothic sculpture fair,
> Did long King Osric's image bear."

It was a large and gracefully designed monument of Perpendicular work of the date of the early years of King Henry VIII., with the effigy of a king, crowned and sceptred.

On the carved stone *loculus* beneath the canopy rested this kingly effigy. The stone figure, somewhat roughly carved, represented an old man with a flowing beard ; lying upon his breast was a model of the Abbey of Gloucester. In black characters of a partly effaced inscription was written :—

### OSRICU⁸ REX [PRIMUS FUNDATOR] HUI⁰ [MONASTERII 681]

The story of the old monarch is as follows :

For three centuries this fair South-west, the country watered by the Severn and the Avon, had been the scene of a quiet, prosperous life, such as was often introduced into the more favoured provinces of the Roman Empire. Gloucester was the great military centre, the place of arms of the West, ever watching the turbulent and uneasy Welsh and Border tribes of the Silures just across the river. Bath was then the famous pleasure city—the watering place of Britain—resorted to by many a sick and ailing legionary and wealthy trader whose duties and fortunes led him to the north of Gaul and the coveted isle across the little silver streak. Splendid villa residences and richly cultivated farms were scattered over the vale and wooded hills. Slowly Christianity made its way in the Severn Lands, but when the end came of the pleasant opulent Roman life, its votaries probably numbered thousands.

In the year of our Lord 577, a terrible calamity befell

south-west Britain. When the Roman legions, the officials and their families, had left Britain finally, about one hundred and fifty years before, in order to defend Italy and the central provinces of the Empire against the vast and ever-increasing hordes of northern tribes, then continually invading in great force the richest provinces of the empire, this part of Britain was evidently in a state of great prosperity and wealth. The important remains of Roman Gloucester and Bath, the splendid pavements and elaborate and luxurious arrangements of the Roman villas in the neighbourhood of these cities, bear witness to the life lived in those far back days. On the withdrawal, however, of the Roman legions in A.D. 409-420, what may be termed the story of Roman life in Britain came to an end. There settled over these districts an impenetrable mist. It seems as though Britain, after the Roman officials and soldiers left, was divided into numerous little kingships. We have of these hundred and fifty years only a few reliques of legendary history—very little dependable. Most probably the old habits of provincial life went on much as before, though on a narrower and less magnificent scale, Christianity, doubtless, gradually winning to its side the great mass of the population. No one seems to have foreseen the danger which threatened these outlying provinces from the northern tribes who had been long plaguing Italy and the south.

It was many years before the awful storm burst on them, but it came at last, and found them, when the shock of battle came, brave but disunited. Ruin and disaster have drawn a dark veil over the ill-fated cities and peoples of these districts.

But through the veil of ruin and disaster we catch sight of one terrible battle fought in A.D. 577, at Deorham (Dyrham), not far from Aquae Solis (Bath), close to the Fosse Road. Ceawlin, grandson of Cerdic the West-Saxon, the Woden-descended, slew at Deorham three of their kings, and took from them three cities, Gloucester, Bath, and Cirencester, banishing or slaying all the old inhabitants. The churches of Christ were everywhere destroyed, and the worship of Thor and Woden and the northern gods replaced Christianity. For nearly a century the Severn Lands completely relapsed into Paganism.

The hero-king, whose canopied tomb stands at the right hand of the altar of Gloucester Cathedral, was apparently the principal agent in the restoration of the lost Christianity of this part of Britain.

The land north of the Humber (Northumberland) had, like the south and west portions of the island, been conquered by the hordes of German invaders; the worship of Woden and Thor there too had taken the place of Christianity. But the Saxon princes of Northumberland were soon persuaded by active and earnest missionaries of the gospel of Christ to give up idol-worship, and the Saxon princes of Northumberland, men like Edwin and Oswald, became ardent worshippers of the "white Christ."

Osric was a prince of their house. He, like his great uncle Oswald, the saint-king of Northumberland, was descended from the conquerors of the northern part of Britain, Ida and Ælla. They, like Cerdic and Ceawlin, the West-Saxon kingly ancestors of our present royal and imperial house of England, boasted their descent from Woden. Osric, too, was closely connected by marriage with Ethelred, King of Mercia and of all the central part of England.

When he was still comparatively young this Ethelred of Mercia, uncle of the young Northumbrian prince, appointed his nephew Osric viceroy or sub-king of the Hwiccian or Severn Lands about the year of grace 681. The Hwiccii were a division or powerful tribe of the West-Saxons.

From notices in early chroniclers—of these Bede was his contemporary—this Osric was evidently something more

than a famous ruler.   He was an earnest admirer of what
was to him and his Pagan race of heroes the new religion of
Christ, and he seems to have used for years his great powers
for its furtherance and establishment.

For many years, as under-king to the great Mercian
sovereign, his uncle Ethelred, he ruled over the Severn Lands,
and his chief work seems to have been the establishment of
a network of Christian fortresses, centres of missionary
activity ; and, after nearly twelve hundred years, several
noble ecclesiastical foundations remain to us as monuments of
his far-seeing religious zeal and earnestness.   In his latter
life this prince succeeded to the crown of Northumberland,
which roughly included Yorkshire and the northern counties.
There he reigned for some eleven years, and, dying in 729 A.D.,
requested to be buried in his abbey of Gloucester.

When the young Northumbrian prince became ruler of the
Severn Lands, the Hwiccii were pure Pagans.    Their kins-
men to the south the Wil-saetas, with the West-Saxon settlers
in Dor-saetan and Somer-saetan, all sacrificed at the altars of
Woden and Thor ; farther away Kent was too distracted
by internal troubles to busy herself with evangelising distant provinces.   Sussex was still heathen.   To the west,
in Wales, still flourished the remains of the old British
Church.   Some eighty or more years before, in A.D. 602-3,
we know that Augustine of Canterbury had met on the bor-
ders of the Hwiccian territory—probably at Aust (Augustine's
oak, opposite Chepstow)—seven Welsh prelates, and many
learned men from Bangor and other religious houses, in a
conference which miserably ended in failure.

But from the Pagan Severn Lands, alas ! this still flourishing Church stood sullenly aloof.*   One who has good right to.

---

* See Professor Bright, "Early English Church History."   See also his
Lecture to the Cathedral Society of Gloucester, 1891 ; and compare a very able
paper by Rev. C. S. Taylor, on "Early Christianity in Gloucestershire" (*Trans.
Glou. and Bristol Archæol. Soc.* xv. 1).

be heard thus sadly writes : " Of any attempt on the part of the British Church to repay good for evil, by evangelising the race which they had too much reason to abhor—the race which had trampled out Christianity in the larger part of our present England—we know nothing at all from authentic history. What was to become of the conquerors as spiritual beings for whom Christ had died?" (In this gloomy but striking passage Professor Bright was speaking with special reference to the West-Saxon Hwiccii of the Severn Lands.)

Surrounded thus on all sides by Pagans, and by a sullen Christian Church who to their shame could not, even for their crucified Master's sake, bring themselves to help the men who in a former generation had desolated their homes and hearths, whence could come to the heathen Severn Lands friendly voices who should tell its people the story of the Christ ? We reply, only from Northumbria, which under the influence of the devoted Paulinus and his noble successors had become in large measure Christian. And from Northumbria it came in the person of Osric, to whom, more than to any man, the dwellers in the Avon and Severn country owe their Christianity. Osric's most enduring work during his long reign in the south-west of England was the establishment of great monastic mission centres, notably at Gloucester and at Bath. Gloucester Cathedral and Bath Abbey are splendid and enduring memorials of his life-work ; Worcester Cathedral too may claim the Northumbrian prince as its first founder. The abbey at Pershore was a foundation of his brother.

His houses were modelled after the famous missionary convent of Streaneshalch (Whitby). There Saint Hild, of the old royal race of Deira, one of the grandest and noblest figures of the seventh century, a near connection, too, of Osric, had on the wild moorland washed by the North Sea built the famous holy house of Whitby. This was one of those strange monastic establishments for missionary purposes peculiar to that age

z

of stern war and burning religious zeal, containing men and women *—admirable in its composition for missionary purposes, but when the first rough work of evangelising was done, this system was discouraged and soon died out. Osric was deeply influenced by Hild and her successor his still nearer relative Ælfleda, daughter of King Oswy, and reproduced the " double " house of Streaneshalch, in Gloucester and in Bath. His sister, Kyneburgh, became Abbess of Gloucester, and Bertana at Bath, and from these and other smaller foundations the broad lands watered by the Avon and the Severn were Christianised.

In comparatively late life, after more than a quarter of a century apparently spent as viceroy of the West-Saxon Hwiccii, Osric succeeded to the great Northumbrian throne. It was a brilliant period of literary activity (considering the age) as well as of Christian missionary zeal, and the court of Northumberland was the real centre of this life in England.

Of this portion of Osric's life we know little or nothing ; still with scarce an exception all the old chronicles with accurate dates tell us he reigned eleven years over Northumbria, and dying in A.D. 729, requested to be buried in his loved abbey of Gloucester, which he had founded nearly fifty years before. William of Malmesbury, writing some four centuries later, speaks of dark scenes which preceded Osric's succession. The same writer tells us, too, that he perished by a violent death. But William of Malmesbury at the same time goes out of his way to speak of the exceeding nobleness of the man.

* Mr. Taylor, " Early Christianity in Gloucestershire," quoted above, remarks on " the frequency of abbesses in these early Hwiccian houses, where a woman ruled over a double community of men and women, the women taking precedence of the men. Archbishop Theodore, in his ' Penitential,' ii. cap. vi. 8, expressed disapprobation of the practice, but as it was the custom of the country, he would not put it away. Certainly it was usual in England at that time. St. Ebba at Coldingham, St. Eldreda at Ely, St. Ethelburga at Barking, Elfrida at Repton, and St. Cuthberga at Wimborne, all presided over double houses of men and women."

St Hilde... Whitby

Google

The reticence here of Bede, who alludes simply to the fact of his occupying the throne at that juncture (the saint-scholar at Jarrow was actually writing his memorable story of England when Osric was king), was possibly owing to his unwillingness to write down any of these dark pages of history while the chief actors in the story were actually living close to his own Jarrow.

All our Cathedral records, dating back many hundred years (Gloucester is very rich in these), unite in bearing witness to the interment of the Northumbrian king within its walls. He seems ever to have been honoured as the founder of the abbey, and yet more as the prince to whose fervour and pious zeal the dwellers in the Severn Lands owe their Christianity.

During the changing fortunes of the religious house of Gloucester the body of its founder Osric appears to have been watched over with anxious care. In the well-known "History" of Abbot Froucester, compiled at the end of the fourteenth century from older records in possession of the abbey, we read that Osric, the king of Northumbria, who died the 9th May A.D. 729, was buried near his sister Kyneburgh, before the altar of St. Petronilla, in the north part of the monastery of Gloucester.

The beautiful canopied tomb of King Osric on the right of the high altar, known as Osric's, is (with the exception of the effigy of the king, which is possibly older) the work of Abbot Malvern, the last Abbot of Gloucester, and stamped with his arms. It occupies the place of honour, the place usually reserved for the founder.

It has been generally supposed to be merely a memorial tomb, simply a cenotaph or empty tomb, probably from the far remote date of the interment of the Northumbrian king 1162 years ago! So Britton, in his great work on the "Cathedrals of England" (vol. v. pp. 66 and 67), speaks of this tomb of Osric's in Gloucester as the "cenotaph." Mr. Waller in his able and exhaustive guide to the Cathedral (edition iii.) repeats the description of the empty tomb which has been universally adopted.

Men of the nineteenth century could not believe that the remains of one who had passed away early in the eighth century were still preserved, still reposed in their midst ! It seemed scarcely credible that even the hallowed dust of the founder could have escaped the ravages of war, time, and neglect; could have escaped the wild forays of the Danish Vikings and the fury of Norman pillage ; could have escaped the confiscations of Henry VIII., and the yet more dangerous watchfulness of Cromwell's Ironsides. So the guardians and custodes of Gloucester Abbey for many and many a year resigned themselves to the firm persuasion that the fair monument on the right of the high altar was but a pious memorial, covered nothing, held nothing—was only a dim and misty memory of a half-forgotten great one! Antiquarian, historian, custode of the great Abbey, all agreed in the conclusion that the tomb of Osric was a mere cenotaph, an empty tomb.

I adopted the tradition of my predecessors, and firmly held this as a part of my Cathedral's story, till one day I met with Leland's record. (Leland was librarian to Henry VIII.) The result of my pondering over this was the solemn night quest, the story of which I am going to tell.

My attention had been called by a fellow-student* to the notes which Leland made in the course of his official visit to Gloucester abbey by King Henry VIII.'s desire, shortly after the Dissolution in A.D. 1540. One of these notes ran thus :—

---

* Mr. Bazley, Rector of Matson—my co-librarian in this Cathedral—an archæologist of learning and research, to whom I am indebted for many a bit of buried lore.

"Osric, Founder of Gloucester Abbey, first laye in St. Petronell's Chapell, thence removed into our Lady Chappell, and thence remooved of late dayes, and layd under a fayre Tomb of stone on the north syde of the high Aulter. At the foote of the Tomb is this written on a Norman pillar, ' *Osricus Rex primus fundator hujus monasterii*, 681.' "

If, now, this was an accurate " memory " of Leland's—and

King Osric's Tomb
*fore Allar steps*

there was no reason to doubt its perfect accuracy, for Leland had heard it
from one of the monks of the fallen
house, from one who probably had
even been an eye-witness of the translation of the founder's
remains from the Lady Chapel—then the canopied monument
in the place of honour in the sanctuary was no cenotaph, no

mere empty memorial tomb, but was in very truth the actual
resting-place of the remains of the great Northumbrian king,
the first founder of the famous abbey.

With these thoughts in my mind I proceeded to consult
Mr. St. John Hope, the secretary of the Society of Antiquaries,
and Mr. Waller, the architect of the Cathedral, and after a
careful examination with me, these experts, with the words of
Leland that I had placed in their hands before them, told me
that the panelled *loculus*, or large stone chest on which the
crowned and sceptred effigy of Osric rested, was amply large
enough to contain another inner *loculus* or mortuary chest.

On the night of the 7th January, 1892, after the Cathedral
was closed, accompanied by Canon St. John the sub-dean, Mr.
Bazley the librarian, the sub-sacrist, two skilled masons, and
Mr. Waller the architect, I caused two panels on the south
side of the stone *loculus* to be removed, and at once a long
leaden coffin was disclosed lying exactly beneath the king's
effigy.    The upper end of the leaden coffin had fallen in,
apparently crushed by the weight of the stone figure of the
king, which was then seen to form the lid of the outer stone
*loculus*, thus exposing to view the contents of the lead coffin.

It was a solemn moment.    The old grey Cathedral was
dimly lit by a few lamps, whose flickering light half-veiled,
half-revealed the mighty Norman pillars of the choir ambulatory, with the delicate lace-work of Perpendicular tracery
carved upon them by the monk-artists of the days of King
Edward III.    The dim gold-work of the sanctuary gleamed
here and there above our heads as the pale shafts of the
lantern lights fell upon the Gothic fancies of the reredos.

It was a weird and striking scene that winter night, as we
stood and silently gazed on the coffin whose existence no man
living had ever suspected—the coffin which held the sacred
dust of the once famous Northumbrian king, who had done
so much in his stormy, work-filled life for his Master's

religion, and who, nearly twelve centuries back, had founded the stately abbey.

The contents of the coffin disclosed the remains of a very ancient interment; much of the cement which had once fastened down the stone effigy of Osric had fallen in to the top or broken end of the lead coffin; a few small bones, or pieces of bones, could be seen mingled with the cement; the lower end of the coffin was perfect, and a grey dust marked the position where the legs and feet of the ancient king had rested. It seemed too hazardous to try and clear away the cement from the upper end of the coffin; it would have disturbed and partly destroyed the mouldering bones. No attempt was made to discover royal insignia or fragments of vesture. The remains were left untouched. The searchers, in their reverent quest, simply desired to test the truth of Leland's assertion that the remains of the body of the great founder of the abbey were there.

Thus in our search we had verified beyond all doubt the statement of Leland in 1540-1, concerning the translation of the body of the royal founder of the ancient abbey and religious house of Gloucester. Owing to our work of that night the stranger, as he passes through the storied church, will in future be told that the fair tomb which occupies the place of honour in the Cathedral is no mere cenotaph, no mere monument raised in pious memory of the founder of the abbey, but is verily the resting-place of the remains of the ancient Northumbrian king to whom, as the restorer of their lost Christianity, Gloucester and the Severn country owe so deep a debt of gratitude. From this night those who love the glorious Cathedral rebuilt by Serlo, Lanfranc's friend, the chaplain of William the Conqueror, will be conscious of another sacred treasure enshrined within the old walls of their loved minster. They will often reverently gaze at the beautiful tomb hard by the high altar—the tomb built up by the pious care of Malvern, the last sad abbot of the great house; and as they gaze they will remember that

King Osric's Tomb
from
Ambulatory
Choir

beneath the carved canopy, beneath the sculptured effigy, rests the hallowed dust of Osric, the Northumbrian king, who, after his stormy life, chose the abbey by the Severn as his last earthly home nearly twelve hundred years ago.

As with the little group of reverent searchers that winter

evening I left the solemn Cathedral, with the dark shadows of night again filling the soaring choir, again resting on the altar, with its stately reredos gleaming with colour and gold, again veiling the tombs of mighty kings and saintly abbots, I reflected on what I and my two or three friends had been gazing : we had seen for a brief moment the mouldering remains of one who had played one of the chief parts in a great and ever-memorable period.

The latter half of the seventh and the early years of the century that followed, when Osric lived and worked, will ever stand out in English history as emphatically a great and memorable age—for it was in those few years that was accomplished the work of our national conversion to Christianity. Our famous historians* love to dwell on the mighty work that was in that brief space of time so well, so surely done. "In a single century," says one of these great writers, "England became known to Christendom as a fountain of light,"† and in the West and Midlands, in our own loved Gloucestershire, it would seem that the master-workman of the great age was Osric.

What thoughts flashed through the busy brain as we slowly passed out through the dimly lit, fair cloister walk, where in old days the Benedictine fathers of the holy house wrote in their little carol cells, quietly waiting the printing press's advent! What thoughts were ours on that cold winter night! Our eyes had looked upon the ashes of one who must have been the friend of Bede—of Bede the saintly, the tireless pioneer of that bright scholar-band who have done so much to train and educate our England. Osric, into whose coffin —the very existence of which none in our day seem to have suspected — on whose mouldering bones we had just been reverently gazing, must have in his youth often talked in

---

* So Church and Freeman, Stubbs and Bright. Alas, the first two have left us!
† Bishop Stubbs.

the cloistered gloom of Streaneshalch (Whitby) with his kinswoman, the saintly Abbess Hild, the friend and counsellor of so many of earth's great ones in that age of brave struggling after light—with Hild who helped to kindle so many a fiery torch of missionary ardour—Hild, the mediæval Mère Angélique,* as she has well been called, "the mother whose advice was sought by princes," and who no doubt sketched out for Osric the scheme for his holy houses of prayer and work on the banks of Avon and Severn.

What thoughts, indeed, what touching memories came crowding into the busy brain after the strange night's work! What a group of friends and counsellors must have been associated with him on whose grey ashes we had just been reverently gazing. Caedmon, somewhiles cow-herd in Hild's home on the wind-swept cliff of Streaneshalch overlooking the North Sea, and then soul-stirring poet after his marvellous awakening to his great gift—Caedmon, the first and not the least illustrious of the long sunny line of English song-men ; Wilfrid, the masterful but devoted bishop who, in his long anxious sorrowful life, never swerved from what he felt was true and just, the spiritual ancestor of Dunstan and Lanfranc, À Becket and Langton—now the champion of the Church's rights—now the wise and loving apostle and teacher of the heathen South-Saxons and the men of the Isle of Wight; Willibrord, the dauntless missionary to the Frisians; St. Chad, the gentle ascetic Bishop of Lichfield; Theodore, the aged archbishop—half Greek, half Roman— with his rare powers of government, his vast knowledge of the Church and the world, his peculiar influence over men's hearts and heads; Colman, the generous and tender Irishman, the brave advocate of the uses of the ancient Celtic Church, the use of St. John the divine ; Cuthbert of Melrose and Lindisfarne, the tireless worker, the loving, patient ascetic,

* Canon Bright.

the ideal of the perfect monk, for ages the great popular
saint of the North Country; Guthlac the solitary, the loved
recluse of the Mercian Lands, whose name still lives among
us in the ruined glories of the mighty abbey at Crowland
in the Fen Country, at once his memorial and his tomb. All
these simple, holy men, whose revered names still shine
among us beacon-like among the framers of our English life,
with many another noble soul in that age of illustrious men,
half forgotten save by a few patient scholars, were, during his
long and eventful life, the teachers and the guides, the friends
and companions of that Northumbrian prince whose coffin I
had just caused to be sealed up once more in his splendid
tomb in the sanctuary of Gloucester Cathedral.

It had been for us a never-to-be-forgotten night. We had
looked upon the hallowed ashes of one who had been a foremost light in the most brilliant period of our ancient
ecclesiastical history—on the ashes of one concerning whom
we may in good truth say, that he was one of the makers of
England.

## Appendix.

(1.) I believe that in the tomb of Osric, Gloucester may
claim the solemn guardianship of the oldest known remains of
the Saxon kings.

Rare fragments exist in other stately minsters. Winchester
possesses in one of its mortuary chests some of the ashes of
Kynegils, King of the West-Saxons, who died A.D. 643, but
the remains of Kynegils are hopelessly mixed with the bones
of Ethelwulph, the father of Alfred. At Durham the skull
of the saint-king Oswald, who died A.D. 634, rests in a
coffin with the bones of St. Cuthbert (the body of the saint-
king Oswald is in Gloucester Abbey somewhere; it was, we
know, brought there by Æthelfleda, Lady of the Mercians, the

daughter of Alfred, in A.D. 909), and possibly the remains of King Sebert, the East-Saxon, rest in the well-known tomb in Westminster Abbey. This, I think, exhausts the scanty list of Saxon kings of an older date than Osric, fragments of whose precious remains are preserved among us.

(2.) Every king and queen who has ruled England before and since the eleventh century has had the blood of Cerdic the West-Saxon, the Woden-descended, in their veins.

Osric's family, the princes of the Northumbrian kingdom, like Cerdic's, claimed to descend from Woden.

The house of Osric, through Oswald, the saint-king of Northumbria, was also allied to the house of Cerdic.

(3.) The lead coffin in which the remains of Osric now rest probably replaces a more ancient stone *loculus* or coffin. The translation from the stone to the lead coffin might have taken place when the remains of Osric were transferred from St. Petronilla's Chapel to the Lady Chapel; or later, in the first years of the sixteenth century, when, as Leland tells us, the remains of the founder of the abbey were taken from the Lady Chapel and deposited in their present place of honour on the right of the high altar " of late dayes"—no doubt by Malvern, Abbot of Gloucester, A.D. 1514—1539, the builder of the tomb, whose well-known arms are carved on the spandrels of the canopy.

# La Grande Chartreuse.

It was in the early spring of 1890 that one night I sat in the cold, bare gallery at the west end of the chapel of the monks of the Grande Chartreuse Monastery. Over the rough wooden balustrade, as I knelt, I looked down on the dim-lighted chapel. The monks, in their white woollen robes, with their white hoods falling over their faces, sat or knelt, each one in his stall. Alternating between chant and prayer and reading, the solemn night service went on.

I had been summoned from the cell allotted to me and had been led by the lay-brother through vast corridors—all silent as the grave, dimly lit and icily cold—into the little strangers' gallery. I had watched the brothers of the Chartreuse glide in one by one noiselessly, each carrying a little lighted lamp. This solemn service, monotonous but yet intensely earnest, went on every night, summer and winter, sometimes lasting two hours, sometimes—on certain holy days—going on for nearly three hours. With the interlude of the Terror, A.D. 1793, and the few years succeeding that time of confusion and dread, had this vigil of prayer and meditation been kept up for more than eight hundred eventful years. The map of Europe had been constructed and reconstructed

—living languages had become dead, had become the solitary property of a few learned and patient scholars ; new tongues had grown up ; new nationalities had sprung into existence ; royal dynasties had risen and fallen ; new peoples had occupied the old seats of almost forgotten races—since the first night of that long and monotonous chant, of that ceaseless prayer of the white-robed, white-cowled fathers of the Grande Chartreuse Monastery, which nestled at the foot of those mighty pine-clad cliffs, towering two or three thousand feet above the solemn city of silence.

Bruno, the founder of this world-famous religious house, was born at Cologne in the year 1035. From childhood he was a lover of books and solitude—a born mystic. His family was noble, and was well-placed to assist the young student in the career of his choice. At a comparatively early age he was appointed a canon of Cologne. Subsequently he became a pupil of the renowned Berengarius of Tours. On the death of Gervais, Archbishop of Rheims, Bruno was designated as his successor. This was the turning-point of his career. The young scholar-mystic had now to elect whether he would become the great Church ruler or pursue his life of solitary contemplation, of study and of prayer.

Lesueur, who died in 1655, in his well-known series of pictures in the Louvre illustrating the life of St. Bruno, reminds us of the legendary cause of Bruno's choice. A famous preacher to whom Bruno loved to listen, and from whom perhaps he learned much of that mystic theology in which he delighted, died suddenly. The remains of this beloved teacher were brought in an uncovered coffin into church ; in the course of the funeral service, while the psalm was being sung, the corpse partly arose, and was heard, in a voice full of intense sadness, to exclaim, " Justo judicio Dei damnatus sum "—I am condemned by God's righteous judgment. To this terrible revelation of a destiny by one whom the young scholar so deeply revered, the legend refers the deliberate choice of Bruno, his unalterable resolve to forsake the world in which lurked so many awful dangers, even for men whose life-duty consisted in ministering at the altar and in teaching holy things. Distrustful of himself, he resolved at once to abandon his preferment, to refuse his call to the high places of the Church, and to realise some at least of his longings after holiness in utter solitude. The legend probably has a basis of truth in it : some overwhelming shock no doubt influenced him and determined his future life. He and six of his dearest friends literally sold, for the benefit of the poor, all that they had, and betaking themselves into the savage solitude of the Chartreuse valley in the neighbourhood of Grenoble, built a little chapel and the first rude group of huts, which rapidly developed into the famous religious house known as the Grande Chartreuse.

*The Grand-Som.*

Aided, no doubt, by the widespread reputation which he had already acquired when he was summoned to become Archbishop of Rheims, the fame of Bruno and his companions rapidly increased. His first company of solitaries was multiplied. In the midst of his success he received a summons, which he could not evade, to Rome, to become the adviser of the Pope, Urban II. After some time again he refused an archbishopric in Italy (that of Reggio) and at length obtained permission to found another company of solitaries in the wilds of Calabria, whose life-work was to be prayer for others, like the first brothers of the order at the Chartreuse, and there this strange mystic, at the age of seventy-one, worn out by austerities, gave up his anxious soul to his Creator.

But his work has been strangely enduring. Throughout Europe the Carthusian order spread. In the beginning of the sixteenth century (A.D. 1521) the number of religious houses owning the stern grave rule of Bruno was 206. Unlike so many of the monastic orders the Carthusian brotherhood never seems to have been reorganized and reformed. Their proud boast was " Cartusia nunquam reformata quia nunquam deformata." This boast appears to have been fairly justified. The historian * of the reign of Henry VIII., in his eloquent and vivid description of the breaking-up of the monastic system in England, speaks of the London Charterhouse, the principal representative of the order of St. Bruno in our island, as bearing (A.D. 1535) a high reputation for holiness, " perhaps the best ordered religious house in England. The hospitality was well sustained, the charities were profuse. . . . The Carthusian monks were true to their vows, and true to their duty." Their house was broken up. The prior, whom Froude describes as " among many good the best," with several of his monks, was publicly executed. The bodies of the monks were quartered, and the arm of the brave prior was hung up as a bloody sign over the archway of the Charterhouse to awe the remaining brothers into submission. Some were done to death in Newgate, and a few escaped abroad. " So fell the monks of the London Charterhouse, splintered to pieces, for so only could their resistance be overcome, by the iron sceptre and the iron hand that held it."

The description of the suppression of St. Bruno's chief house in England nearly five centuries after the foundation of the Grande Chartreuse, by a pen by no means friendly to the spirit of the monastic orders, is a striking testimony to the enduring character of Bruno's work. No passage perhaps in

* Froude, vol. ii., chap. ix.

that picturesque and brilliant story of our great historian is more eloquent and moving than the words in which he describes the Carthusian monks of London, A.D. 1535, preparing for their violent and shameful death. " Thus with unobtrusive boldness did these poor men prepare themselves for their end, not less beautiful in their resolution, not less deserving the everlasting remembrance of mankind, than those three hundred who in the summer morning sat combing their golden hair in the passes of Thermopylæ : we will not forget their cause; there is no cause for which any man can more nobly suffer, than to witness that it is better for him to die than to speak words which he does not mean. Nor in this their hour of trial were they left without their higher comfort."

It was a dreary, melancholy evening when I first caught sight of the pointed roofs and curious towers of the great monastery. It had been raining heavily for several hours, and the lofty cliffs were veiled in masses of soft grey, feathery clouds. The damp wind whistled through the pine forests;

no other sound was heard, nothing living was to be seen.
The monastery, with its vast extent of high walls, with its
quaint blue roofs and many towers rising up behind the walls
in strange, fantastic confusion, with its gloomy background of
dark pine woods, resembled a fortress, or what would be a
better comparison still, one of those small walled cities so often
depicted in illustrated MSS. of Froissart or Monstrelet.   I
knocked at the north gate, the chief entrance to the Grande
Chartreuse.   A white-robed lay-brother (*frère convers*) opened
it, and received me with some kindly words of welcome.
Through the great silent porch we passed into a wide inner
court.   Not a flower, not a plant relieved the grey melancholy
monotony.   Two little fountains, with their monotonous drip,
drip, alone broke the intense stillness.   From the broad
courtyard we passed into a wide, chilly corridor, apparently
of endless length, then into a hall with a welcome wood fire.

I had a letter of introduction to the general of the order,
who always resides at the Grande Chartreuse.   He sent me
a courteous message that he would receive me early on the
following morning, and that in the meanwhile I was to receive
every hospitality and attention which the laws of the order
permitted.   An immense wood fire was lit in the guests' refectory (*pavillon d'Allemagne*), and a little cell leading out of
the refectory hall was allotted to me.   The furniture of my
cell consisted of a narrow bed with its thick woollen cover-
lets, a chair, and a *prie-dieu.*   Its only ornament was a rough
wooden crucifix over the *prie-dieu.*   A little window, looking
into a long and desolate courtyard in which the snow lay thick
(it was early in April), lighted my chamber.   No one could have
been kinder than my hosts.   They brought me everything they
had, eggs, and some little dried figs and withered apples, and
a curious, tasteless fish—I think with more bones than any
ordinary fish possesses—and soup which was at all events
warm though it had no taste.   The delight of the lay-brother

when he spread these tempting viands before me was curious.
" You see," he said, " we do not expect our honoured guests to
fast." There was wine, a rough, harsh Burgundy, and some
admirable green Chartreuse, very aromatic and of extraordinary strength. But the hearty kindness and the warmth
of the welcome made up for any lack in the quality of the
viands.

" Hospitis adventu gaudent . . . .
Dant quod habent, hilari pectore, voce, manu." *

After the repast I told the lay-brother I wished to
be present at the night service, and then retired to my cell.
It was very cold and damp in my little narrow sleeping-cham-
ber, in spite of the great wood fire which burned cheerily in
the neighbouring refectory, so I wrapped myself up in my rug,
and slept fitfully for two or three hours. About a quarter of
an hour before the night service they fetched me, and placed
me in the strangers' little gallery overlooking the chapel. The
chapel is a long, narrow building, very plain, and unadorned.
The rood-screen divides it into two portions. The fathers
occupy stalls in the eastern division, the lay-brothers stalls in
the western. The strangers' gallery is in the extreme west
end of the building, and commands a fair view, over the rood-
screen, of the whole chapel.

The time passed quickly as I listened to the sweet, monotonous chant, varied with reading. In the pauses of the
solemn song I heard these solitaries, forgotten by the world,
praying for the world. " I heard them interceding for men who
at that moment of the dark night were forgetting God and
truth, purity and goodness. I heard the murmur of the solemn
petitions which had gone up to the throne of grace night after
night for many centuries, prayers for the poor and the wretched,
for the guilty and the crime-laden, for the dying and the dead,
for the faint-hearted that they might hope again in God, for

* From a Carthusian poem of the twelfth century.

the light-hearted lest they might forget God." It seemed to me as I listened and prayed too, that to these men thus talking with the Master had come, in the silence of their cloistered lives, that whisper of the Eternal, the " vena divini susurri," which taught them the secret of the language of communion with God, which even dictated the words of those earnest, passionate prayers by which these solitaries believed they could best help their brothers and sisters struggling and suffering in the world. . . . Were they mistaken in their strong, simple faith ? I think not.

At last the lay-brother begged me to go back to my cell. He said I was not accustomed to the cold, damp air of the chapel, and if I stayed longer it would be dangerous. With real reluctance I went back with him, and when I stood again before the refectory fire I felt how thoroughly chilled I was with my night's orisons. However, I soon slept, and awoke early in the morning none the worse.

One of the strangest things in this solemn night service is the monotony, the sameness of the chant. The Carthusian liturgy, with little change, dates from the eleventh century. The singular monotony of the singing has been the subject of much inquiry. Their ancient statutes notice it, and suggest the following *apologia* for it :—

" Seeing that the life-work of a true monk is made up of weeping rather than singing, let us use our voices to win for the soul that inward joy which comes from tears, rather than for those emotional feelings which are produced by sweet and touching music. With this goal in front of us, let us eliminate from our singing and music everything which may have a tendency to produce these emotional feelings, which are frivolous—perhaps even wrong. . . . Our music must consist of a chant—at once simple and full of devotion."

One of their famous masters thus dwells on the subject :—

" The intense gravity of the solitary's life does not allow much time to be devoted to the study of singing."

St. Jerome too is quoted by the Chartreuse apologist here as laying down a rule for the monk's life :—

"It is no solitary's duty to teach, much less to sing. His life work is to weep over his own and the world's sins, and with fear and trembling to look for the Judge's awful advent.'

Many of the strangers who attend their services find no fault with this sameness and monotony ; on the contrary, they find it produces a singular feeling of deep calm and intense seriousness.\*

Petrarch, who listened to the Chartreuse service in 1353, speaks of their psalmody as being in very truth "angelic."

One not very far removed from our own times wrote somewhat in this fashion of his impressions of their grave and austere night worship :—

"In the dim, scarcely lit chapel from those white kneeling figures, each with his little lighted lamp, there rose up the strange, solemn, chanted psalm. As they sang, the attentive listener could even distinguish the powerful notes of the monk still in the vigour of life and the broken voice of the worn-out old father, fast nearing the haven where he longed to be. The Psalms have thus been sung and the earnest prayer prayed in the solemn night service for many centuries. Death has been powerless to empty those dark stalls where the white monks have prayed and prayed for nearly nine hundred years."

Some six times has the great house been destroyed : once by an avalanche, once sacked and ruined in the religious wars of the sixteenth century, four times it has been the prey of a disastrous fire. The present monastery is a little more than two hundred years old ; but it almost exactly reproduces a much older house. It contains long, bare corridors leading to ample accommodation for representatives from the Carthusian · houses founded in every part of Europe, once numbering between 200 and 230, now, alas, mostly suppressed and ruined. Their priors, yearly, with certain of the brothers of their houses, meet in solemn conclave at the Grande Chartreuse. Portions of the great house are still named after the various

---

\* I felt no weariness in the long service, and was very sorry when the lay-brother, owing to the intense cold, begged me to return to my cell. The service in question on that night was unusually long, it was one of the great Carthusian festivals.

countries of their illustrious guests—the Pavillon d'Italie, de Bourgogne, d'Allemagne, de Provence and d'Aquitaine, &c. There are a vast number of chambers for many guests, who in all times have been welcomed to the Grande Chartreuse.

The ordinary dwellers in this city of silence consist of thirty-six fathers, twenty-five lay-brothers, and some 120 servants; many of them, save in the guest season, probably have work in the farms, liqueur distillery, and other dependencies of the house. There is a fine chapter-room, several council-chambers, and a really noble library. The two churches or chapels are studiedly plain and unadorned. The stranger, as he passes through the seemingly interminable corridors, silent, apparently untenanted, white and cold, can scarcely repress a shudder as he contrasts his life, with its many interests, enjoyments, excitements, with the austere and silent existence of these men who have buried themselves in this remote and changeless solitude.

By far the most interesting part of the monastery is the cloister and its immediate surroundings. It is of immense length—nothing of the kind in France can be compared to it in extent—a considerable portion of it is of real beauty, and dates from the fourteenth and fifteenth centuries. The cells or, more correctly speaking, the houses, of the thirty-six monks or fathers, open directly into these cloisters. Each cell is now filled, and I was informed there were many waiting for a vacant cell. Each cell or house is complete in itself, and stands alone, a little plot of garden separating it from its neighbour. The door of each house or cell opens into the cloister. Each door, following the old practice of the solitaries of the Thebaïd, is marked with a letter of the alphabet, and also with an inscription, selected usually from the Bible, the "Imitation," or a well-known Father. The monk chooses this device on the day of his pronouncing his last solemn vows. The device may be said to sum up and to close his earthly career. I copied a few of these—

" Domine dilexi decorem domus tuæ."
" Vanitas vanitatum."
" Quam angusta porta et arcta via quæ ducit ad vitam, et pauci sunt qui inveniunt eam."
" Domine si sine te nihil, totum in te."
" Qui non reliquit omnia sua non potest esse discipulus tuus."
" Sobri simplices et quieti."
" O beata solitudo—O sola beatitudo."

By each door there is a small sliding shutter in which is placed the daily allowance of food and anything else they may have special need of. Should they require aught, they place a written memorandum specifying their want, in the opening by the shutter, and it is at once supplied to them.

No brother-monk, no friend in the cloistered community ever passes through the close-barred door of the Chartreuse father's house. The monk comes through it to certain of the daily services, and on Sundays and festival days to the common refectory, and once in the week to the public walk (*spatiamentum*), but when, after the service or the silent Sunday or festival meal, he crosses his threshold, he is absolutely alone. I was permitted to inspect one of the houses. The monk was temporarily absent from his little home, administering, I believe, the last rites to a dying brother. I passed the door ; within on the ground floor is a little gallery or exercise hall, where the solitary paces up and down during the long months of winter and of snow, when his own patch of garden ground is inaccessible. The garden, which he cultivates himself, is very small and cramped ; in some cases it is exquisitely neat, in others comparatively neglected ; it is really the Chartreuse father's sole recreation. Another room on the ground floor he uses to chop his wood in. The wood is abundantly supplied to each monk in large, rough logs. This he prepares for his fire as he pleases. Up a rough flight of

*The House or " Cell" of a Father of La Grande Chartreuse.*

(*From a print in a work on the Order, published by a monk of the monastery.*)

stairs, or rather of steps, the real dwelling-place is reached
—the home where the Chartreuse father spends so many
lonely hours. It is divided generally into two chambers. The
one is little more than an ante-room, with usually a very small
study-room cut off from it. The second chamber contains a
kind of cupboard which holds the comfortless-looking bed,
with the rough blanket-rugs which form the bedding of this
austere order. By the bedside are a little chair and *prie-dieu*
and crucifix, where so many of the Church offices are said by
the lonely monk, for it is only three of the services that he
says in the public chapel of the monastery. His silent room is
really his chapel. The recess of the window is his refectory,
and is partly filled by a little table. The great refectory is
only used by the monks on Sundays and on certain festival
days. The study is the small room taken from the ante-
chamber. Again in this little corner of his quiet home the

furniture is of the scantiest, simplest description—a table, a
rough desk, and a few shelves against the wall filled with
the books for daily use and the volumes borrowed from the
noble library of the house.[*]

Into these secluded cells within cells no servant is permitted to enter, the fathers do all that is to be done themselves
—*la solitude dans la solitude*, as one of the Chartreuse fathers
has called the little quiet house, in which no voice is ever
heard, save his own, into which enters no friend or foe. Many
a world-weary man, once owning a high and distinguished
name,[†] many a great scholar, statesman, or soldier, has here
passed the evening—not a few the midday too—of their once
stormy, eventful lives; prayer, thought, study, meditation, filling up the rapidly-passing hours.

> "Tu mihi curarum requies, tu nocte vel atrâ
> Lumen, et in solis tu mihi turba locis."—Tibul. iv. *Eleg.* xiii.

Francis de Sales found these lines painted round such a
cell as I have described.

Thomas à Kempis once wrote how he sought everywhere
"heart-rest," and he had only found it in a corner with a book
—*in angulo cum libro.*

À Kempis too said the longer the monk lives in his cell
the dearer the cell becomes to him—*O beata solitudo—O sola
beatitudo!*

The library of the Grande Chartreuse is a large and noble
apartment, and though shorn of many of its former cherished
treasures, is still rich in literature of various kinds and ages,
theology by no means occupying the only place on its well-
lined shelves. The fathers have the freest access to these

---

[*] "Les livres sont l'impérissable nourriture de nos âmes."—Guigues le
Vénérable, 5th General of the Order, A.D 1109.

[†] In the cloister I passed a monk, his cowl drawn over his face. My guide (the
*frère convers*) whispered me as we passed the father that in the world that
monk was known as "Prince de B.," mentioning one of the great names of
France. In those silent ranks are men once of renown as generals, statesmen,
writers, engineers, &c.

books, and may either use them in the public room, or take them—as they in most cases prefer to do—to their own well-loved cells.

Part of the long cloister walk surrounds a garden—the garden of the dead. There in the little enclosure have been buried for centuries the monks of the famous house. There is nothing beautiful or attractive in this most solemn of God's acres; the Carthusian ever sternly repudiates beauty in his surroundings. The very landscape, in the midst of which his great house is built, is repellent in its gloomy grandeur and sombre colouring, while the monastery is severely plain, and would be deemed even ugly, were it not for the strange charm which hangs round everything connected with the Grande Chartreuse—the sweet charm with which unbroken centuries of self-denial and generous self-forgetting prayer for others invests this holiest of monastic centres.

In this God's acre are little brown wood crosses, each marking the last home of a monk—crosses which rapidly disappear, and are as quickly replaced by the same holy symbol marking the sleeping place of another monk. The remains are uncoffined, and soon disappear in the dry earth of the Chartreuse valley.

From twenty to thirty stone crosses, some carved more or less elaborately, not a few dating back several centuries, mark the graves of the generals of the order. But there is no care bestowed even on these memorials of their great dead. It is the immortal soul alone that the Carthusian cares for, and in death as in life he pays little heed to the perishing body. But a stranger naturally feels disappointed and saddened at this studied neglect of all beauty, even of all ordinary care, in this most holy ground where the ashes of the dead of centuries rest. While acknowledging their utter disregard for the remains of the poor perishing body to be a natural outcome of the austere Carthusian teaching, it must

The Cloister

be confessed that the neglected God's acre of the Grande Chartreuse is depressing and saddening even to the reverent admirer of these very noble, even if mistaken men.

The night service we have spoken of is the longest and most remarkable in their daily routine; it lasts never less than two hours, often on festal days three hours and over. The fathers say this is their happiest time, singing, praying, reading, in God's holy sanctuary, in the deep hush and awful shadows of night, a time when the world forgets God, or too often sins against Him. They say these solemn hours win for the soul a joy indescribable, a peace for the soul so profound that no price is too great to pay for it. They tell us how quickly the night hours pass when they are thus busied.

Mr. Froude, in his striking paraphrase* of Maurice Chamney's story — he was one of the last monks of the London Charterhouse (A.D. 1535) — gives us what was no doubt then, is probably still, an average picture of the feelings of a Carthusian father respecting the life he had voluntarily embraced. Chamney was a monk who, accepting King Henry VIII.'s clemency, escaped the martyr's death, which was the high guerdon of so many of his nobler companions, and in after years Maurice Chamney wrote his confession of bitter sorrow for his earlier apostasy. He speaks of his cowardice in the day of battle. He was doing a life-long penance in sorrow, tossing on the waves of the wide world, while his brother-monks—the martyrs for God—were saints in heaven. He draws a loving, lingering picture of his cloister life, to him the perfection of earthly happiness. Here is his moving story: "It lies before us in all its superstition, its devotion, and its simplicity, the counterpart, even in minute details, of accounts of cloisters when monasticism was in the young vigour of its life, which had been written ten centuries before. . . . The prayer, the daily life . . . seemed all unaltered; a thousand years of the world's history had rolled by and these lonely islands of prayer remained still anchored in the stream."

Maurice Chamney's picture of the London Charterhouse would have done for a picture of the Grande Chartreuse which I visited in 1890; and his estimate of such a

* " History of England," vol. ii. chap. ix.

cloister life being "a life of perfect happiness" would, as far as I can gather, be the estimate of the present generation of the fathers of the Grande Chartreuse of to-day.

The solitude is only broken on Sundays and festal days, when the fathers of the house take their principal meal together in the refectory, but on these occasions they never speak.

The silence is only broken once a week, when the daily routine is interrupted by a long walk (*spatiamentum*) which the fathers take together.

The cold and damp of the climate of these mountains necessitate very warm clothing. The dress of the monks of the Grande Chartreuse, quaint and simple as it seems, is only the ordinary costume of the peasants of the mountains of Dauphiny in the eleventh century, and was adopted by Bruno, the founder of the order, as the most useful and least costly. It is all made of wool and is entirely white. The white robe closely resembles the *tunica talaris* (reaching down to the heels) of the Roman provincial. This is fastened by a white leather belt. Over this goes a white woollen toga or cloak, slit at the sides to allow free play to the arms. The head is covered with a white woollen cowl.

The mystic writers on the great monastic orders tell us that while St. Benedict, loving especially to dwell in thought and teaching upon the death of our blessed Lord, adopted for his disciples a black habit, St. Bruno elected white for the habit of his monks, to symbolize our Lord's resurrection, which he is said to have loved continually to meditate on and to speak of.

The number of fathers of the order in the Grande Chartreuse is limited to thirty-six, the number of cells or separate little dwellings. This number is never exceeded.

The entrance into the famous company is rigidly guarded. The postulant is first received by the master of the novices, who begins his duties by washing the feet of the new comer. He then, after due examination, presents him with a great black cloak, which he always wears when not in the cell during his probation. This lasts a month, or perhaps more, under certain circumstances. He then commences his formal novitiate. This lasts a year, sometimes longer. He is next presented to the chapter, who formally vote for the admission or rejection of the novice. If the scrutiny of votes is in his favour, he is vested in the Carthusian habit.

But he does not take his solemn life-long vows until four years after this ceremony.

The final profession is a great solemnity; it takes place during high mass. The monk who is taking his final leave of the world leaves his stall, and at the foot of the altar thrice chants, " O my God, receive me as Thou has promised, and I shall henceforth live the true life. O God, let me never be confounded." Then he kneels down before each of the fathers, and says to each, " My father, pray for me." Then he receives the rest of the habit which hitherto he had not worn, and takes the solemn, binding oath; he proceeds to kiss the altar, and to lay upon it the writing of his solemn profession, signed, not with his name—he has no longer any name—but with a cross, for he is dead to the world.

A modern Carthusian writer speaks of the life of his order as a life of solitude, but of solitude alternating with occasional commune with his brethren ; as a life of prayer, but of prayer varied with work—now of the brain, now of the hand. He speaks of it as an austere life in real earnest, but disfigured with no painful or exaggerated incidents. " God," writes this enthusiastic and eloquent advocate of his renowned order —" God pours the dew of His blessing on an order in which the grave wise rule of our founders preserves a peace which the world cannot give."

The Carthusian monk is a student. Before the art of

printing, he was often a diligent scribe ; he is still often a profound scholar; he has in no few instances been a painstaking author ; he is reproached at times with the strong reproach of writing only to tear up and destroy his own compositions. Little, say his gentle critics, has ever issued from beneath that white cowl save hymns and psalms of praise to his God, and prayers for the unhappy and the suffering in the world which he has left for ever.

The especial work of the monks of the Grande Chartreuse is not the care of the sick and afflicted; but they maintain homes for the suffering poor, their revenues being sensibly augmented by the great sale of their famous liqueur, manufactured at a distillery a few miles distant from the monastery, and into the composition of which many herbs growing on the slopes of the Alps largely enter. The secret of the liqueur is rigidly kept.

But the *raison d'être* of the life of a monk of the Chartreuse without doubt is prayer. Such a life, where all is sacrificed for this one end, may not be our ideal of life surely. The busy man of the nineteenth century seeks more definite, more tangible results than the Carthusian father. He would aim at the blessed guerdon of the honoured philanthropist, at the laurels of the great soldier, at the applause ever given to the successful writer. The solitary believes that only in the silence of his cell he can do his best, his truest work, for he knows that there the Friend of Friends is ever with him in his awful solitude. Never comes the question :—

> "Why doth He come not ? Wherefore should He come,
> Who never from my side can go away ?
> His is the first face seen when dawns the day,
> His the voice heard when birds sing or bees hum,
> And His the presence felt when night is dark and dumb."

He asks for nothing for himself ; in God who fills his cell he has everything. So he prays for others living in that sad,

restless world which lies outside his quiet garden of prayer
men call the Chartreuse.

Our loved poet puts the same thought into the heart of the
dying king, when Arthur from the dusky barge says to his
faithful knight—

> " Pray for my soul.   More things are wrought by prayer
> Than this world dreams of.   Wherefore, let thy voice
> Rise like a fountain for me night and day.
> For what are men better than sheep or goats
> That nourish a blind life within the brain,
> If, knowing God, they lift not hands of prayer
> Both for themselves and those who call them friend ?
> For so the whole round earth is every way
> Bound by gold chains about the feet of God."

" I consider," said a thinker of our own times, " that, after
all, those who pray do more for the world than those who
fight, and that if the world is gradually growing more corrupt,
it is because there is more fighting here than praying.   If we
could but discern the secret things of God and of history, I
am sure we should be amazed at the mighty results of prayer
in all human matters.   In order for society to be at peace,
there must exist a certain equilibrium (God alone can deter-
mine what that should be) between prayers and acts, between
the active and the contemplative life.   My belief is—and here
my belief passes into certainty—that if on any given day one
hour were allowed to pass without a prayer going up from
earth to heaven, that day and that hour would be the last for
our world."*

Who among us that believe in the mighty power of prayer
would dare to cast a stone at these devoted men, who, in
pursuit of what *they* deem the highest ideal of life, have given
up all that men hold dear—home, friends, love, rank, fame,
ease, comfort.   They have voluntarily cast all these prized
things aside, and only live their grave, austere, perhaps joyless

* Donoso Cortès.

lives, to help, in the way they deem most effective, their suffering, erring neighbours.

 *         *         *         *         *         *

Some may perhaps wonder why the writer has closed his series of studies of "Cloister Life in the Days of Cœur de Lion" with this little nineteenth-century picture of a cloister where the old life is still lived in all the fair beauty of renunciation and self-sacrifice, and intense faith in the power of prayer, which Hugh of Lincoln, Cœur de Lion's friend seven centuries ago, showed to be so possible—so full of blessing.

It is true, quite true, that

> " The old order changeth, yielding place to new."

But have not men in the restless stir and feverish excitement of modern times lost a *something* which in the rough days of Cœur de Lion often helped and invigorated world-weary souls, and gave them fresh strength to fight anew the hard life-battle ?

The Chartreuse life may be, probably is, an anachronism, but it suggests, if it does not positively teach, a beautiful lesson which earnest men may well lay to heart ; it seemed therefore well to tell its story.

Some of us—students of a past which, with its many evils and sorrows, was still possessed of elements of a deep peace and real happiness unknown to us now—may at times regret, with a regret surely not misplaced, the silence of those " sweet bells of convent and monastery heard in the evening hour, charming the unquiet world to rest and remembrance of God."

www.ingramcontent.com/pod-product-compliance
Lightning Source LLC
Chambersburg PA
CBHW030822270326
41928CB00007B/856